American Mosaic

American
Mosaic

AFRICAN-AMERICAN CONTRIBUTIONS

The History of African-American Colleges and Universities

Jennifer Peltak

CHELSEA HOUSE
PUBLISHERS

A Haights Cross Communications Company

Philadelphia

Frontis: Students attend a class at Morehouse College in Atlanta. The school was founded in 1867 by William Jefferson White, and is still one of the premier black colleges today, comprising the "black Ivy League" with such schools as Spelman College, Howard University, and Hampton University.

CHELSEA HOUSE PUBLISHERS

VP, NEW PRODUCT DEVELOPMENT Sally Cheney
DIRECTOR OF PRODUCTION Kim Shinners
CREATIVE MANAGER Takeshi Takahashi
MANUFACTURING MANAGER Diann Grasse

Staff for THE HISTORY OF AFRICAN-AMERICAN COLLEGES AND UNIVERSITIES

ASSOCIATE EDITOR Benjamin Xavier Kim
PRODUCTION EDITOR Jaimie Winkler
PICTURE RESEARCHER Pat Holl
COVER AND SERIES DESIGNER Keith Trego
LAYOUT 21st Century Publishing and Communications, Inc.

A Haights Cross Communications ◀ Company

http://www.chelseahouse.com

First Printing

1 3 5 7 9 8 6 4 2

Library of Congress Cataloging-in-Publication Data

Peltak, Jennifer.
   History of African American colleges and universities / Jennifer Peltak.
       p. cm.—(American mosaic)
Includes index.
Summary: A comprehensive look at historically black colleges and universities, from their origins to the present time, including the individuals and groups involved in creating that history.
   ISBN 0-7910-7269-X HC   0-7910-7492-7 PB
   1. African American universities and colleges—History—Juvenile literature. 2. African Americans—Education (Higher)—History—Juvenile literature. [1. African American universities and colleges. 2. African Americans—Education (Higher) 3. Universities and colleges.] I. Title. II. Series.
LC2781.P39 2003
378.73'089'96073—dc21

                                            2002155105

Table of Contents

A classroom from 1906 at the Tuskegee Institute in Alabama. This school was founded by Booker T. Washington in 1881, providing one of the earliest sources of education for blacks.

Uplifting the Race

At the heart of historically black colleges and universities, otherwise known as HBCUs, lies the ideal that education is for all, regardless of color and class. The concept of a universal education has long been implicit in the values of America. However, the history of black colleges and universities reveals that higher education has often been reserved for the few, the wealthy, and the white. Both law and tradition have, until recently, largely excluded black men and women from attending white universities and colleges. As a result, a dual system of higher education arose to educate blacks.

Historically black colleges and universities refer to more than schools with a predominately black population. Rather, they are a small group of schools founded before or after the Civil War and prior to the Civil Rights era anointed by *Brown v. Board of Education* in 1954. The four million slaves freed by the Emancipation Proclamation in 1863 sought equal rights after the Civil War, including education. Black colleges and universities were established throughout the South by the federal government and religious denominations.

However, the specter of racism persisted throughout the country, especially the South. The U.S. Supreme Court upheld laws allowing states to separate blacks and whites. The majority of historically black colleges and universities are a product of this segregation. These schools provided an education when few other opportunities for black students existed. Today there are 103 HBCUs in 17 states, the District of Columbia, and the Virgin Islands. They are typically small schools with enrollments ranging from a few hundred to around 8,000 students; 53 are private and 50 are public. Prior to 1991, HBCUs awarded 71 percent of all degrees earned by black students. They educated future lawyers, doctors, dentists, farmers, and teachers decades before white schools were forced to open their doors. There are also 54 predominately black colleges and universities, or PBCUs, in the U.S. Unlike HBCUs, predominately black schools opened after 1954, usually without the specific mission of educating black students.

Historically black schools have developed in a unique fashion. The oldest institutions for higher learning in the United States—Harvard and Princeton, for instance—followed the European model of higher education. They accepted students based on their academic excellence or their wealth. This exclusive arrangement has never been an option for HBCUs. In fact, HBCUs have always been highly sensitive to barriers of race and class that can discourage students from pursuing their goals. The earliest black schools served a population without any advantages. At the start of the Civil War, for instance, just 10 percent of the slave population could read or write. The simple goal of the first black colleges was to teach newly freed slaves how to read and write. The mission of HBCUs has been defined as "not who gets in but what happens to them afterward." The mission statement of Norfolk State College in Virginia summarizes this egalitarian approach to education, stating "A person's innate right to improve himself through access to education must never be governed by his socio-economic status or his background, whether these be disadvantaged or not."

While historically white schools required a certain level of knowledge and experience from their students, serving an educated population was a goal but not a reality for the earliest black schools. As a result, the tradition at black schools is to meet the varied expectations and experiences of black students. In his book *The Evolution of the Negro College*, Oliver Wendell Dwight Holmes points out that "at the beginning of the Civil War, the Negro, generally considered, began his academic education at zero. . . . The cultural level of the constituency of Harvard and of William and Mary . . . was far different from and in general far above that of the freedmen in 1863. The colleges for Negroes are unique, therefore, among American institutions of higher learning."

The history of HBCUs can be reasonably divided into three periods. The first era, from 1837 to 1890, begins with Cheyney University in Philadelphia, the oldest historically black school in America. A wealthy Quaker founded the college with the mission of creating black teachers. In the North, free blacks were able to receive limited educations, usually from religious societies, and small numbers attended white universities and colleges. Two other black colleges opened before the Civil War, Wilberforce College in Ohio and Lincoln University in Pennsylvania. The South, which depended on slave labor to maintain its economic system, encouraged a racist view of blacks as ignorant savages undeserving of education. Many white Southerners believed an educated slave would encourage revolution. Educating slaves was outlawed, and those slaves who did learn how to read and write often did so in secret, usually from sympathetic owners or other whites. The chaos of the Civil War, however, allowed Northern missionary societies to tour the South, teaching slaves how to read. The missionaries believed that the path to saving souls began with educating the mind.

Four million slaves were free by the end of the Civil War in 1865. To meet their pressing needs, the federal government established the Freedmen's Bureau, which had the task of supplying shelter, land, education, and assistance to former slaves. By the time the bureau disbanded in 1872, it had founded over 4,200 schools. Religious groups also founded numerous private colleges throughout the South after the Civil War. The majority of these public and private schools could not be defined as traditional colleges and universities. Many were "normal" schools that educated teachers; others were industrial schools that prepared blacks for practical trades or simply provided an elementary education. Some schools, such as Howard University in Washington, D.C., and Fisk University in Tennessee, did establish college departments for students to pursue advanced degrees.

The growth of a black college system in the South, however, was slow and often encountered great resistance. The federal government appeased the situation with the Morrill Land-Grant Act of 1890. This act prohibited federal grants for colleges and universities to states that did not integrate or include facilities for black students. Rather than integrate, white Southern governments allowed colleges and universities serving the black population to charter. The majority of HBCUs, also known as land-grant schools, formed as a result of the Morrill Act.

The second era for HBCUs, from 1890 until 1954, was a time of segregation between blacks and whites. In 1896, the U.S. Supreme Court upheld the rights of states to separate blacks and whites as long as "separate but equal" facilities were provided. This ruling allowed a parallel system of education to develop that would last until the Supreme Court ordered states to desegregate schools in 1954. Thus, the majority of HBCUs organized in an era when race relations were still highly volatile. Black schools, for the first few decades of their existence, were colleges and universities in a loose sense. In *The Evolution of the Negro College*, Holmes writes that "the Negro land-grant colleges as a group have followed, in general, the same pattern of development, which consists in the beginning with elementary studies along with strong emphasis upon agriculture, trades, and teacher training for work at the

Students at Hampton Institute (later renamed Hampton University) making bricks in 1899. Founded by Samuel Armstrong, one of its most prominent alumni was Booker T. Washington, who used Hampton's focus on industrial education as a model for his own philosophy on higher education for blacks.

lower levels, followed by a gradual raising of standards in teacher-training courses to higher levels."

One of the earliest and most successful HBCUs was Hampton University, then called Hampton Institute. The institute very much embodied its era. The founder, as with many HBCUs, was a white man, Samuel Armstrong. He believed that a practical education rooted in the industrial arts would improve the quality of life for blacks while making them valuable to white employers. His most famous pupil was Booker T. Washington, who later founded the Tuskegee Institute using his mentor's model of industrial education.

A number of the new HBCUs offered a liberal or classical education to students. Washington believed this to be largely a wasted effort. He "viewed education mainly as a utilitarian enterprise aimed at self-sufficiency and economic prosperity." In other words, learning French would not help the newly freed slave; a skill in brick-making or farming would. At a time when most HBCUs taught an elementary education, Washington's philosophy seemed prudent. Less concerned with civil rights and black disenfranchisement, Washington urged blacks to make concilia-tory gestures toward white Southerners and apply themselves to practical trades. His views gained him much fame and support among white Southerners and Northern philanthropists.

However, a growing number of black scholars faulted Washington's philosophy for limiting opportunities for black people. Only an education of the mind, they argued, would lift black people from a servile mentality. Washington's most astute and famous critic was W.E.B. DuBois, a professor at Atlanta University. Born free and educated at Fisk University, a historically black college, and Harvard University, DuBois "favored a program of education that would teach the Negro to think." A strong advocate of civil rights, DuBois argued that without an education in math, English, history, foreign lan-guages, and the arts, blacks would not be able to challenge white supremacy. DuBois' views influenced many HBCUs to raise their academic standards. Until World War II, Washington's and DuBois' views dominated the direction of HCBUs. By the 1960s, DuBois' ideology was more accepted than Washington's. Many HBCUs had dismantled their agriculture and industrial programs by the time of the Civil Rights era in favor of the classical education DuBois described, although a respect for practical schooling is still evident today.

As HBCUs matured, governments and philanthropists took note. Several surveys between the first and second world wars attempted to document the progress of HBCUs. The surveys pointed out the great disparity between HBCUs in their curriculum and value of degrees. Also, despite the "separate but equal" doctrine, the black industrial schools of the South were often inferior to their white counterparts. One study revealed that black schools received one-fourth the public funding enjoyed by white schools. These surveys had two lasting results. One, HBCUs became an acceptable fact of higher education, and their contributions were acknowledged. Black schools began to fight for more recognition. The Southern Association of Colleges and Schools, founded in 1895, begin working with black colleges in the 1920s. In 1931, 31 black colleges received permission from the American Medical Association to start pre-med programs. And by 1930, "the great majority of HBCUs had developed into full-fledged colleges, had dropped non-college courses, and were requiring all entrants to have high school diplomas."

The second result of the surveys was increased attention to the financial health of HBCUs. W.E.B. DuBois had noted that "passing the hat" remained the acceptable way to fund black schools. Churches and missionary societies had provided the bulk of support for black schools. By World War I, a new group of secular organizations—including the Rockefeller Foundation, the Julius Rosenwall Fund, the Phelp-Stokes Fund, and the Carnegie Foundation, contributed money for improving the quality of HBCUs. When funding became scarce during the Great Depression and World War II, a group of private black colleges banded together to form the United Negro College Fund. They appealed for donations and divided the collected funds. In its first year the fund raised $765,000, "a sum three times larger than that raised by the individual colleges in separate campaigns in previous years."

The third era of historically black schools begins in 1954, when the U.S. Supreme Court declared segregated schools to violate the rights of black Americans. The next two decades saw tremendous changes on black campuses. Predominately white colleges and universities competed for the best black students and faculty, causing a so-called "brain drain" on black campuses. The students who remained at black schools agitated for a greater say in academic affairs. They chafed against outdated requirements and demanded a more radical curriculum. They believed black men and women should run black schools, not whites. They wanted more black faculty. Sit-ins and protests were a common sight on black campuses throughout the 1960s and early '70s.

Despite the turmoil on black campuses, the 1960s and '70s saw a brighter financial outlook for HBCUs. The Civil Rights Act and the Higher Education Act of 1965 opened federal aid for historically black schools and scholarships for black students on an unprecedented level. States that did not provide funding to historically black schools were denied federal funds.

Many historically black schools redefined their mission over the past two decades, some as elite, research-based institutions such as Howard University and Spelman and Morehouse colleges in Atlanta. Others reached toward a deprived population, "including many who require remedial training, and expose this group of students to resources they would not otherwise receive."

Historically black colleges and universities now serve a much smaller population. In 1990, historically black schools enrolled just 28 percent of all black students. Enrollment did rise at HBCUs between 1976 and 1990 by 10 percent, but black enrollment at white institutions rose 20 percent in the same period. Statistics paint a fairly positive picture of HBCUs. Surveys of black campuses have also shown that students are more successful at predominately black schools rather than white campuses. Students describe a close relationship with faculty, a sense of comfort among fellow black students, and an absence of racist attitudes as crucial to their success. One study found that black students at black schools are twice as likely to finish college as black students on predominately white campuses. The confidence that black students find on black campuses is reflected in their choice of major. For instance, students at black colleges were twice as likely to major in business, engineering, and the sciences than students at white colleges. Despite the historical antipathy toward black colleges and universities, these schools have

Vivian Malone, the first African-American student at the University of Alabama, walks on campus in 1963. The end of segregation not only caused friction with the admittance of black students into previously all-white colleges, but also was responsible for drops in attendance at historically black schools.

succeeded in creating a black middle class with the means "to maximize their economic potential."

Like the missionary groups that reached out to slaves during the Civil War, historically black colleges are as concerned with lifting the spirit as they are educating the mind. Students who embrace black colleges find encouragement they may lack elsewhere in society. A student at Fayetteville State University in North Carolina concluded, "A lot of black people don't know what they can become. You find out at black colleges."

An original drawing for the book *Uncle Tom's Cabin* depicting a slave market. Even though slavery eventually became outlawed, the attitudes of racism would still hinder African Americans' quest for equality and the opportunity to obtain education.

2

The Origins of African-American Education

In 1837, the first college for black students opened in Philadelphia. It was not a college in the traditional sense; in fact, children of all ages received instruction. Their classes prepared them to become teachers so that they could teach the next generation of black students. It was a humble beginning for black higher education in America. Barely two centuries after America was colonized, slavery was already an entrenched institution in the young republic. Africans had been imported as slaves to work in the fields and homes of white settlers since the earliest days of the country. Although America's founding fathers led the country to independence from Great Britain and declared "life, liberty and the pursuit of happiness" to be a cornerstone of the struggling democracy, freedom did not extend to slaves.

Education was a priority in the new world. Harvard University opened in 1636 and Princeton 90 years later; the first state university was chartered in 1781. In 1785, the Continental Congress passed a law preserving public lands for the support of free schools, which declared: "Religion, morality, and knowledge being necessary to good government and the happiness of mankind, schools and the means of education shall forever be encouraged."

Prior to the Civil War, roughly four million acres of federal land were allotted to states to build universities, and 60 million acres were set aside for free schools. The schools were intended solely for white students. It would be nearly 100 years after the Declaration of Independence was written before black citizens would be able to form their own colleges and universities. Once the doors to education opened, however, many students were eager to take advantage. Within two decades after the Civil War, over 100 colleges and universities for black students had chartered. Their purpose was to provide a basic education for newly freed slaves to read, write, and learn practical skills. As the needs of students evolved beyond basic literacy, many of the schools developed a liberal arts or industrial curriculum. In essence, educator and social scientist W.E.B. DuBois wrote, black colleges and universities provided the important transition between slavery and freedom.

CRISIS OVER SLAVERY

The U.S. Constitution does not explicitly mention slavery, but references to it are found throughout the document. The framers included the "three-fifths clause," which counted slaves as three-fifths of one person, in order to secure the South extra representation in the House of Representatives. Another clause required runaway slaves to be returned to their owners and gave the government power to put down rebellions, including slave insurrections. Founding Fathers such as Ben Franklin and Alexander Hamilton argued that slavery was hypocritical and unjust, especially for a country that was founded by those fleeing oppression. When they wrote the Constitution, the framers knew they had failed to adequately address the already-contentious issue of slavery, but such concessions were considered necessary in order to secure the support of Southern delegates to the Constitutional Convention. Without those concessions, it was feared not all states would join the new Union.

The clauses are a small part of the Constitution. Still, leaders such as James Madison knew the issue would have to be resolved, and that it would be a great test for the young democracy, saying that "It seems now to be pretty well understood that the real difference of interests lies not between the large and small but between the northern and southern states. The institution of slavery and its consequences form the line of discrimination."

SLAVERY LIFE AND "BLACK CODES"

After the Revolutionary War, the Northern states gradually outlawed slavery. In the South, however, slavery was the backbone to a vast farming economy. Estimates vary, but it is thought that up to 10 million slaves were brought from Africa. In the first U.S. Census in 1790, 700,000 slaves were recorded. This number mushroomed after 1798, when Eli Whitney invented the cotton gin. The cotton-growing plantations could now farm cotton at a much faster pace, which led to an increased demand for slave labor.

Life for most slaves was brutal and dehumanizing. Slaves were often stripped of their names, their families, and their individuality. Cultures and languages disappeared in the new and hostile world. Efforts to resuscitate the dignity and value of slaves—establishing new families or educating one another, for example—could be brutally punished. Slave revolts, such as the one led by Nat Turner in 1831, frightened slave owners. To squash potential rebellions, Southern states enacted "black codes." Slave owners believed that slaves who could read and write were responsible for the rebellions. As a result, "harsh laws forbidding the instruction of Negroes in reading, writing and arithmetic were passed as a defensive measure throughout the South." Due to this suppression, it is estimated that not more than 10 percent of the slave population could read or write at the time of the Emancipation Proclamation.

The black codes and brutal conditions of slave life made education difficult, though not impossible. Educator and former slave Booker T. Washington, in his autobiography, *Up From Slavery*, noted that he never knew when or where he was born. Claiming their history was a secretive and rebellious act for slaves.

"Of my ancestry, I know almost nothing. In the slave quarters, and even later, I heard whispered conversations among the coloured people of the tortures which the slaves . . . suffered . . . while being conveyed from Africa to America," Washington wrote. "In the days of slavery not very much attention was given to family history and family records."

RESISTANCE AND THE QUAKERS

Naturally this unjust system did not go unchallenged. A growing number of white Americans deplored the inhumane treatment of blacks. Those who fought to dissolve slavery were known as abolitionists. They argued that blacks were entitled to many of the same rights as white citizens, including the right to an education. Many of the early abolitionists were part of a religious group known as the Quakers. As early as 1688, a group of Quakers protested slavery in Pennsylvania: "From the earliest days, slavery in colonial America troubled the consciences of Quakers . . . Quakers permitted slaves to attend their meetings." Quakers believed in social equality between men and women, poor and wealthy, and between races. Therefore, for Quakers to hold another person as a slave violated the tenants of their religion.

Although they had once been slave owners, Quakers voted to outlaw slavery among themselves in 1776. Their efforts to uproot slavery did not end there. Quakers formed anti-slavery groups, pressed state legislatures to outlaw slavery, spoke out in public

The invention of the cotton gin increased demand for slaves in the South. In order to keep down rebellions, slave owners forbade slaves from learning how to read and write. These would become known as the "black codes."

against slavery and worked in secret to deliver runaway slaves to freedom via the Underground Railroad. The Pennsylvania Abolition Society, formed by Quakers, included Ben Franklin, Noah Webster, and Thomas Paine among its members. Their aim was to give aid to free Negroes and "establish schools for Negroes whenever possible." One Quaker, Anthony Benezet, started a night school in his Philadelphia home in 1750 and taught black students for 20 years.

Prior to the Civil War, education for blacks was basically nonexistent. The reasoning against educating blacks was highly contradictory. Blacks were considered to be intellectually inferior. At the same time, white Southerners believed an educated slave would be more likely to rebel. The fear of educated blacks was a "persistent phobia" in the South. In the early part of the 19th century, no white schools in the South accepted black children. There were some exceptions. Two schools for black students operated in Virginia up to a decade before the Civil War. Berea College in Kentucky admitted black students despite near-constant persecution from angry whites. After the bloody rebellion led by John Brown in Harper's Ferry, Virginia, Berea's founder was accused of endorsing slave rebellion. The school was then "threatened by a mob and the whole college community was compelled to flee for safety across the Ohio River."

The hostility toward black education was common throughout the South. One teacher in Norfolk, Virginia, was imprisoned for teaching black children. In *The Life and Adventures of an American Slave*, Henry Bibb recalled that slaves were not allowed pens, paper, or anything "to improve their minds." When a white girl in the neighborhood decided to teach slaves how to read, "this caused quite an excitement in the neighborhood. Patrols were appointed to go and break it up the next Sabbath."

Life for freed blacks also had no shortage of hardship. Educational opportunities were somewhat better in the North, but racism and poverty persisted. Oberlin College in Ohio admitted black students. The African Free School for elementary-age children opened in 1787 in New York City. Within 40 years, the school received public funding. But other communities were less eager to assist in the education of black children. In Connecticut, a Quaker woman opened a school for black girls. Opposition to her efforts was virulent. Locals attempted to burn down the school and a state law was passed forbidding the free education of blacks. Overall, very few blacks in the North received enough education that would allow them to attend white colleges or universities.

Blacks in the South largely relied on benevolent whites for even the most paltry of educations. Abolitionist Fredrick Douglass began his education when the wife of his master taught him how to read and write a few words. When Douglass' master found out, he forbade his wife to instruct their young slave further, stating that an educated slave would no longer obey his master. And he was not entirely wrong. Once Douglass had a brief taste of education, he felt like a different person. As he wrote in his autobiography, "From that moment, I understood the pathway from slavery to freedom."

Instead of obeying his master, Douglass secretly enlisted the children of his poor white neighbors to continue his education. He took to carrying scraps of bread for payment for his unlikely tutors. "This bread I used to bestow upon the hungry little urchins, who, in return, would give me that more valuable bread of knowledge," he wrote.

THE FIRST BLACK COLLEGES

Although abolitionists were divided over the role free blacks ought to play in American society, they understood that education was key to delivering slaves and poor free blacks from misery and struggle. When white Quaker Richard Humphreys arrived in Philadelphia in 1764, he witnessed poor blacks struggling for jobs and opportunities. Race riots in 1829 convinced Humphreys to change his will and designate $10,000 to establish a school for blacks. After Humphreys' death, 13 Quakers were charged with

Abolitionist Frederick Douglass managed to overcome the education-denying "black codes" by asking the children of white neighbors to tutor him. He would "pay" them for their instruction with bread.

forming an institution " . . . to instruct the descendents of the African Race in school learning, in the various branches of the mechanic Arts, trades and Agriculture, in order to prepare and fit and qualify them to act as teachers." In 1837, 24 years before the start of the Civil War, the school opened in Philadelphia as the Institute for Colored Youth.

The Institute for Colored Youth—later to be renamed Cheyney University of Pennsylvania—was not a college in the strictest sense. The institute educated children of all ages, with an emphasis on preparing students to become teachers. The earliest black colleges focused on teaching trades over a classical education. For practical reasons it was thought that blacks should have skills that made them valuable to employers.

Prior to the Civil War, two more private colleges opened to teach free blacks—Lincoln University in Pennsylvania and Wilberforce University in Ohio. Like many of the black colleges and universities that opened after the Civil War, Lincoln and Wilberforce were both sponsored by religious denominations; Lincoln as a Presbyterian school and Wilberforce as a Methodist Episcopal school. Higher education for blacks, however, was a rarely glimpsed dream prior to the Civil War. Only a handful of black men received advanced degrees prior to the Civil War.

In the decades leading up to the Civil War, opposition to slavery grew increasingly vehement. The industrial economy of the North did not require slaves while the plantations of the South were entirely reliant on slavery. Books such as *Uncle Tom's Cabin* fueled white outrage over the inhumane treatment of slaves. Congress enacted several laws aimed at quelling the tension between the North and South by balancing the number of states that allowed slavery and the number that were "free." But the political divide deepened, particularly over the issue of whether to allow slavery in the new Western states. Shortly after President Lincoln's election in 1860, South Carolina seceded from the Union, and within several months the country was at war. At issue was the economic direction of the country and the future of its enslaved black population.

The Civil War managed to be a fruitful period for black education. Beginning in 1861, missionary groups from the North laid the groundwork for a formal system of higher education for blacks. The American Missionary Society led these efforts, establishing seven black colleges and 13 teaching schools between 1861 and 1870. The missionaries were not necessarily abolitionists; they were concerned with lifting the spirits of the slaves and saving their souls. They believed education was key to improving the lives of slaves.

Once the Union Army began occupying Southern territory, slaves fled to the newly emancipated land. In some cases, military leaders protected the slaves and missionaries were allowed to open schools for blacks in the territory. Despite the efforts of missionaries and some well-meaning military leaders, the missions encountered great difficulty. Southern whites attacked the missionaries as well as the blacks. The federal troops committed acts of violence against freedmen while army officials stole supplies and generally undermined the efforts of the missionaries.

In 1863, Lincoln issued the Emancipation Proclamation, ending two-and-a-half centuries of slavery in the United States. Two years later, the Union Army declared victory over the Confederacy. The era of Reconstruction had begun.

Reconstruction—the period of rebirth and rebuilding follow-ing the Civil War—was a very important time in the history of black colleges and universities. The era of Reconstruction, which lasted from 1865 to 1877, saw the Northern states attempting to restore relations with the South. "Reconstruction" also refers to the rebirth of the country and the intent to include all of its citizens—black and white—in the democracy. Nearly all of the schools now known as Historically Black Colleges and Universities (HBCUs) formed during Reconstruction.

With the end of the Civil War, there were now roughly four million freed slaves, known as freedmen. Many could not read and write and had no way to provide for themselves or their families. The South was now the home for the majority of black Americans. In the 1900 census, nearly 90 percent of black Americans lived in the South. Immediately after the Civil War, missionary societies and other benevolent groups flooded the

South to helped with the "immediate and pressing need," according to Holmes. He went on to write, "Almost every religious sect and many other philanthropic organizations, aroused to the highest pitch of missionary zeal . . . rushed to the South to give succor of all kinds to the freedmen wherever the need seemed greatest."

The federal government quickly involved itself, too. To assist the newly freed slaves and displaced whites, Congress founded the Bureau of Refugees, Freedmen, and Abandoned Lands, also known as the Freedmen's Bureau. The bureau, which lasted from 1865-1872, gave food and supplies, set up hospitals, resettled displaced blacks and poor whites, and founded over 4,200 schools.

According to black activist and educator W.E.B. DuBois, in the nascent years of Reconstruction, the Freedmen's Bureau wielded a great deal of power. He wrote, "The Freedmen's Bureau became a full-fledged government of men. It made laws, executed them and interpreted them; it laid and collected taxes, defined and punished crime, maintained and used military force . . . 'scarcely any subject that has to be legislated upon in civil society failed, at one time or another, to demand the action of this singular Bureau.'"

But it was the free schools formed by the Freedmen's Bureau that were, in DuBois' eyes, its greatest success. According to DuBois, by 1870, 150,000 black children were in school. Besides the missionary societies and the Freedmen's Bureau, blacks themselves were initiating schools. Known as sabbath schools or African schools, this network of schools operated in "church basements, private homes, warehouses, and pool rooms, and shacks." The sabbath schools were often funded by black donations; by 1879, "blacks by themselves had expended over $1 million on private school education." Overall, the bulk of financial support for schools founded in this period came from the Freedmen's Bureau, the American Missionary Society, and a variety of church groups.

A Freedmen's Bureau school located in Edisto Island, South Carolina, circa 1865. This bureau, set up by the government from 1865 to 1872, provided many services to freed slaves and displaced whites. One such service was setting up free schools, attracting many potential students.

Black students flooded the new schools, and in some cities in greater numbers than white children attending school. In 1865, 75 of the black children in Washington, D.C., attended school while only 41 of white children did. In Virginia, 82 percent of black children received schooling. The education of black children and adults remained bitterly opposed in some quarters. Dismantling the system of slavery did not, of course, eradicate the racism that had become its own institution. In Charleston, West Virginia, no white family would offer a room to teachers who educated blacks. Another teacher in Tennessee was flogged and driven out of town for teaching blacks. A teacher in Kentucky drove a black teacher out of the county and destroyed the school. Antipathy to blacks worsened in the waning days of Reconstruction when white Southerners took hold of local governments. In 1865 and 1866, many Southern governments enacted laws known once again as the black codes. Some codes prevented blacks from owning land or established a nightly curfew for blacks. Berea College, which admitted black students again after the Civil War, was forced to dismantle in 1904 by a Kentucky law forbidding blacks and whites from attending college together. "The opposition to Negro education was bitter in the South, for the South believed an educated Negro to be a dangerous Negro," W.E.B. DuBois wrote in a 1901 issue of *The Atlantic Monthly*.

The U.S. Supreme Court affirmed this entrenched racism. In the 1896 case *Plessy v. Ferguson*, the Court supported the rights of state governments to separate blacks and whites. In this ruling, the court allowed states to separate facilities—including schools—for blacks as long as they were "equal" to white facilities. In fact, conditions for black students were usually separate and unequal. One study indicates that in the Southern states, government spending on black students amounted to one-fourth of the amount spent on white students. The "separate but equal" doctrine, however, remained in place until the Supreme Court declared segregation to be unconstitutional in 1954.

THE MORRILL ACT AND LAND-GRANT COLLEGES

The devastation of the Civil War resulted in the disenfranchisement of many whites and blacks. Education, particularly in the South, cracked along racial and class divides. Although the Constitution had been amended to guarantee a public education for all, white leaders in the South were not eager to educate blacks or poor whites. In 1862, Senator Justin Morrill led a movement to improve higher education in the United States. Morrill's solution emphasized a need for practical education in the applied sciences, agriculture, and engineering. Born poor, Morrill once said, "My sympathies are all for the workingman, being one myself and with all my kith and kin of that sort." He fought Southern opposition to the act until 1862, when the Southerners who had seceded from the Union could no longer oppose the measure.

The Morrill Land-Grant Act donated federal lands to the states to open colleges and universities for farmers, scientists, and teachers. Though many schools opened under the act, blacks were not encouraged to start schools or attend them, especially in the South. Only one school, Alcorn State University in Mississippi, was created as a black land-grant school. The task of educating blacks fell mainly to the Freedmen's Bureau and the American Missionary Society (AMS). The AMS founded seven black colleges and 13 teaching schools between 1861 and 1870, including Fisk University in Tennessee and Morehouse College in Atlanta. Many African-American churches also ran their own schools, primarily for elementary education.

Clearly more than good intentions would be necessary to integrate former slaves into society. To combat the racism that persisted after the Civil War, Congress passed the 14th Amendment in 1866, which gave full citizenship to blacks and guaranteed that all laws would apply equally to blacks and whites. Access to higher education for blacks greatly improved under the second Morrill Land-Grant Act of 1890. Under Morrill's revision, schools using federal land-grant funds had to either open their doors to blacks or allocate money for segregated black schools. Many whites, particularly in the South, were not willing to attend school with blacks. Rather than integrate, most states chose to fund exclusively black schools. In 1890, 16 black institutions received money to start schools for higher learning. Between 1870 and 1910, state governments founded over 100 black colleges and universities.

Senator Justin Morrill was the driving force behind the Morrill Land-Grant Act of 1862 (and a second incarnation in 1890), which made federally funded schools open their doors to blacks, or set money aside for segregated black schools.

The surviving original colleges and universities are today's historically black colleges and universities. All of the original black colleges and universities were founded at the time of the separate but equal doctrine, meaning blacks and whites would be segregated but, in theory, have equal educations. This was often not the case, as white colleges and universities received more funding from the state and were more likely to receive money from alumni and wealthy donors. While the land grants provided the initial funds, schools often scraped by, relying on charity, dedication, and occasionally good luck.

SPELMAN COLLEGE

Spelman College illustrates the good luck and pluck necessary to found a black college. The founders of Spelman College, an all-female college in Atlanta, were fortunate enough to have an encounter with billionaire industrialist John D. Rockefeller. Sophia B. Packard and Harriet E. Giles were commissioned in 1879 by the Woman's American Baptist Home Mission Society to study the living conditions of freedmen in the South. According to a Spelman biography, the two friends were "appalled by the lack of educational opportunities for Black women" and decided to start a school. In 1881, they opened Spelman in the basement of a Baptist church with just $100 provided by another Baptist church. The 11 students—ten women and one girl—were ex-slaves who wanted to learn how to read the Bible. The dedicated women toured churches, trying to raise money for their new school. At a meeting in Cleveland, Ohio, they were introduced to Rockefeller, who gave them everything in his wallet and pledged more if they showed true dedication, saying, "There are so many who come here and get us to give money. Then they're gone, and we don't know where they are—where their work is. Do you mean to stick? If you do, you'll hear from me again."

Within two years, Packard and Giles managed to relocate the school to a nine-acre site. They raised money from the surrounding black community and teachers volunteered their time, relying on contributions of clothing, supplies, and furnishings. On the third anniversary of the school, Rockefeller returned, and was so impressed by what the women had accomplished that he settled their debt.

What black schools and universities lacked in equal treatment, they made up in dedication to their students and a commitment to education, regardless of hardship. Although most HBCUs were founded to provide elementary instruction or train teachers, several—including Atlanta, Fisk and Howard—founded college departments by 1872. Historically black schools such as Morehouse College and Spelman College in Georgia opened in church basements. These schools accepted everyone, regardless of income or prior education. Because many of the founders of historically black schools had recently been born into slavery or seen its horrors firsthand, they rejected the idea that school should only be open to an elite few. Ingrained in the history of historically black colleges is the idea of education as a right, not a privilege.

Booker T. Washington was one of the major figures in the early debates on black education. His philosophy on education stressed the industrial aspect, rather than introducing a traditional liberal arts education.

3

The Debate Over Black Education

As black colleges and universities matured and prospered, educators questioned how best to educate black students. Should their education be focused on practical skills or a classical education that emulated white universities? Embedded in these questions was a debate over the future of black men and women in America. The two leading voices in this debate were Booker T. Washington and W.E.B. DuBois. For several decades the two men and their differing philosophies dominated black education and shaped the path of black colleges and universities.

In his autobiography *Up From Slavery*, Booker T. Washington describes his shock and wonderment at overhearing two miners discuss a college for blacks in Virginia:

This was the first time that I had ever heard anything about any kind of school or college that was more pretentious than the little coloured school in our town. . . . I heard one tell the other that not only was the school established for members of my race, but that opportunities were provided by which poor but worthy students could work out all or a part of the cost of board, and at the same time be taught some trade or industry. As they went on describing the school, it seemed to me that it must be the greatest place on earth.

The school was the Hampton Normal and Agricultural Institute. Washington was determined to go. He managed to save a small amount of money before setting out for Hampton. Along the way he walked and begged rides. Washington finally arrived in Richmond, Virginia, about 82 miles from Hampton, penniless and exhausted. A ship captain gave him a job and Washington slept outside to conserve his meager earnings until he was able to travel again.

"I reached Hampton, with a surplus of exactly fifty cents with which to begin my education," wrote Washington. "To me it had been a long, eventful journey; but the first sight of the large, three-story brick school building seemed to have rewarded me for all that I had undergone in order to reach the place. . . . I felt a new kind of existence had now begun—that life would now have a new meaning."

Hampton was, at the time Washington attended it, an agricultural and normal school. "Normal" was the term at the time for a teaching school. Nearly all of the earliest black colleges and universities were either agricultural or normal schools. Spelman College, for instance, instructed students on subjects such as sewing, cooking, and millinery.

Formed in 1868, Hampton had implemented a successful system of industrial education. The definition of industrial education is a matter of debate, but it encompasses manual training in tools and machinery for the purpose of agricultural and industrial labor. At the time, an industrial education was thought to be a practical outlet for blacks struggling for survival in white society. In 1853, Fredrick Douglass wrote a letter to Harriet Beecher Stowe advocating the goals of an industrial college "where [black students] can be put in possession of the means of getting a living whether their lot in life may be cut among civilized or uncivilized men."

As black colleges and universities opened after the Civil War, the direction of the curriculum became pertinent once again. At the time, it was thought that learning trade skills rather than a liberal arts education would make the newly freed black population attractive to white employers. Such a philosophy was pragmatic given the limited opportunities blacks had at the time, but it was also based somewhat in notions of black inferiority.

The industrial program was very successful at Hampton. Washington's mentor at the Hampton Institute was Samuel Armstrong, a white man who headed the institute and had commanded black troops during the Civil War. Armstrong's views on the value of providing a practical education to blacks greatly shaped Washington's philosophy. Armstrong believed an industrial education would "replace . . . stupid drudgery with skilled hands." In his autobiography, Washington wrote that his time at Hampton taught him to appreciate manual labor and the sense of independence it can foster:

> Before going [to Hampton] I had a good deal of the then rather prevalent idea among our people that to secure an education meant to have a good, easy time, free from all necessity for manual labor. At Hampton I not only learned that it was not a disgrace to labour, but learned to love labour, not alone for financial value, but for labour's own sake and for the independence and self-reliance which the ability to do something which wants done brings.

In time, Washington's views became a philosophy. In his essay "The Awakening of the Negro," Washington describes seeing a poor black boy studying French grammar in a broken-down cabin, and meeting a young woman who lived in utter poverty, yet her parents scraped together money for piano lessons.

"Some one may be tempted to ask, Has not the Negro boy or girl as good a right to study a French grammar and instrumental music as the white youth?" wrote Washington. "I answer, Yes, but in the present condition of the Negro race in this country there is need of something more." He later describes coming across a student who was studying banking although the student did not have experience with banking. He wrote, "I had to summon a great deal of courage to take a student who had been studying cube root . . . and explain to him that the wisest thing for him to do first was thoroughly master the multiplication table."

In Washington's view, "it seems to me that too often mere book education leaves the Negro young man or woman in a weak position." He advocated practical courses that would lift the spirit of workers once they mastered a particular skill.

"Many seem to think that industrial education is meant to make the Negro work as he worked in the days of slavery," wrote Washington. "This is far from my conception of industrial education. . . . It consists of teaching him how not to work, but how to make the forces of nature—air, steam, water, horsepower, and electricity—work for him."

Though Washington was born a slave and witnessed slavery's horrors, his work as an educator led him to form many alliances with white people and to seek their support for his efforts. When Armstrong was asked to recommend a white man to open a new black college known as the Tuskegee Institute, he recommended Washington. The Tennessee school opened with Washington as its head in 1888. According to one Washington biography, "The school taught academic subjects but emphasized a practical education. This included farming, carpentry, brickmaking, shoemaking, printing and cabinet-making. This enabled students to become involved in the building of a new school. Students worked long hours, arising at five in the morning and finishing at nine-thirty at night."

Washington began devoting more time to fundraising, a task that increased his prominence, particularly in white society.

A history class at the Tuskegee Institute in 1902, the school founded by Booker T. Washington. While there were academic subjects taught at Tuskegee, most of them focused on subjects like carpentry and brickmaking.

Tuskegee became known nationwide as a model for industrial education. Socially, Washington was conservative, preferring that blacks should tirelessly work without protest or agitation in order to prove their loyalty. His views—that blacks should be satisfied with a humble trade—appealed to white Southerners and the rich Northern donors whose pockets Washington hoped to reach, but also to poor blacks, who saw Washington's view as a way out of poverty.

In *Up From Slavery*, Washington recounts that local whites were very hostile to the opening of Tuskegee. He invited the community to purchase bricks from students, and when the whites saw the high-quality bricks offered by Tuskegee students, Washington wrote, it quelled many of their suspicions. Washington recalled that

> Many white people who had no contact with the school, and perhaps no sympathy with it, came to us to buy bricks because they found out that ours were good bricks. They discovered that we were supplying a real want in the community. The making of these bricks caused many of the white residents of the neighborhood to begin to feel that the education of the Negro was not making him worthless, but that in educating our students we were adding something to the wealth and comfort of the community.

Known as "the Tuskegee Idea," Washington's popular views secured the Tuskegee Institute many donations. Indeed, most of the early black colleges focused on teaching trades and preparing schoolteachers over teaching French grammar and managing bank accounts. Because of his moderate social views, Washington was perhaps the best-known black leader in the country, and he took great pride in being accepted in white communities.

WASHINGTON'S CRITICS AND W.E.B. DUBOIS

But other black educators were finding flaws with Washington's rhetoric. They did not believe that blacks had to be subservient to whites in order to eventually earn their rights. The great disenchantment with Washington's goals came after his speech at the Cotton States Exposition in 1895. Known as the "Atlanta Compromise," Washington described the black race as five fingers separate in the areas of social progress but united as a hand for mutual progress. Though praised by whites, in the black community the speech was interpreted as "black acquiescence in disfranchisement and social segregation if whites would encourage black progress in economic and educational opportunity."

In 1901, Washington had a historic meeting with President Teddy Roosevelt at the White House. Much of his time was now spent on the lecture circuit, speaking on the educational and financial opportunities for black people while ignoring the issue of civil rights. If Washington's views on education provided the first major model for historically black colleges and universities, it was his greatest critic, W.E.B. DuBois, who provided the next model for black educators and students. Washington's conception of education as an economic tool was crucial for the birth of black schools, but it was DuBois' fiery rhetoric and belief in cultivating black minds to their fullest that provided the foundation for the next generation of black schools and universities.

DuBois, one of the fiercest critics of racism prior to the Civil Rights movement, was born after the Civil War in 1868 in Massachusetts. He attended Fisk University, a black college in Tennessee, and in 1895 became the first black man to receive a doctorate from Harvard University. While at Harvard, DuBois studied philosophy, but his interest shifted to the economic and social problems of black Americans. As one of a few black students, DuBois felt isolated at Harvard. His comment about the school, "I was in Harvard but not of it," captured the continued appeal of black colleges and universities. That is, the welcoming and accepting tradition of black colleges has been as important as intellectual pursuits for generation after generation of students.

In 1896, DuBois undertook a research project in Philadelphia's poorest neighborhoods. At the time, he believed that there was a "cure" for racism that could be found through intensive research. The outcome of his exhaustive efforts was "The Philadelphia Negro," which debunked DuBois' own beliefs about assimilation. Though he had once "believed that social science could provide the knowledge to solve the race problem, he gradually came to the conclusion that in a climate of virulent racism . . . social change could be accomplished only through agitation and protest."

W.E.B. DuBois was a critic of Washington's philosophy on education, believing that its accomodation would only perpetuate racism. One of the founders of the NAACP, he thought that blacks should rise above the industrial model of education in order to be on equal footing with whites.

This was the direct opposite of Booker T. Washington's philosophy of accommodation and patience. As DuBois saw it, outlawing slavery and adding amendments to the Constitution could not cure a racist society where lynchings were not uncommon and segregation laws were accepted. Washington's views, according to his best-known critic, "rather than freeing the black man from oppression, would serve only to perpetuate it."

As DuBois' views gained prominence, leaders of the black community split into two wings, Washington's "conservative" supporters and DuBois' "radical" critics. DuBois believed that educated blacks—those who had received a classic college education—were best suited to lead the battle against racism.

DuBois was not opposed to the industrial education that Washington had pioneered. He expressed great admiration for Washington for rising out of slavery, educating himself, and dedicating his life to educating blacks. Industrial education, DuBois said, provided a necessary bridge between slavery and freedom. In his essay, "Of Booker T. Washington and Others," DuBois stated: "One hesitates, therefore, to criticize a life which, beginning with so little, has done so much."

But DuBois abandoned his reservations: "There is among educated and thoughtful colored men in all parts of the land a feeling of deep regret, sorrow, and apprehension at the wide currency and ascendancy which some of Mr. Washington's theories have gained." Washington came to prominence during Reconstruction, when hard work and rapid economic development were the focus of the country. Washington's philosophy was shaped by that context, DuBois argued, going on to say that "Mr. Washington's programme naturally takes an economic cast, becoming a gospel of Work and Money to such an extent as apparently almost completely to overshadow the higher aims of life. . . . Mr. Washington's programme practically accepts the alleged inferiority of the Negro races."

DuBois was not shy in his criticism of Washington. He characterizes Washington's efforts to placate Southern white fears as "propaganda." The Hampton-Tuskegee model of industrial education worked in its era, DuBois said, but it was not the future of black colleges and universities. He also said of Washington, "He advocates common-school and industrial training, and depreciates institutions of higher learning; but neither the Negro common-schools, nor Tuskegee itself, could remain open a day were it not for teachers trained in Negro colleges, or trained by their graduates."

In a speech at Fisk University, DuBois mocked some of the humbler aspects of industrial education: "The milking of cows is a worthy industry but it is not a cultural study upon which any honest college can base its bachelor's degree." The black college should take a loftier view, he said. "The great chemical and physical laws which underlie the making of many food products are matters which could profitably be treated in a college course."

Until Washington's death in 1915, he and DuBois exchanged barbs in print and in speeches. Washington criticized the establishment of the National Association for the Advancement of Colored People, of which DuBois was a founder. Although Washington secretly funded civil rights lawsuits, in public he expressed views that were popular with white Americans, and continued to be an ally of powerful white politicians until his death.

DuBois taught at Atlanta University from 1897 to 1910. In speeches and books, he further crystallized his theories on the future of black education. In "The Education of Black People," a series of ten essays, DuBois defines education as "fundamentally subversive. . . . and that education [is] part of the process of liberation for his people." Each essay consists of a speech given to a black college, and DuBois is often sharply critical of his audience. His belief that black colleges could liberate the mind informed his pointed criticisms. In the preface, DuBois calls higher education "the true founding stone of all education."

"Such a race must have thinkers and leaders," wrote DuBois, "and for the education of all these folk we need good and thorough Negro colleges."

Unlike Washington, DuBois believed the young boy who studied French in his shack to be a future black leader that colleges and universities should nurture. In a speech at the Hampton Institute in 1906, DuBois criticized it for relinquishing the duty of educating black minds. He wrote, "The aim of the higher

THE CRISIS

A RECORD OF THE DARKER RACES

Volume One NOVEMBER, 1910 Number One

Edited by W. E. BURGHARDT DU BOIS, with the co-operation of Oswald Garrison Villard, J. Max Barber, Charles Edward Russell, Kelly Miller, W. S. Braithwaite and M. D. Maclean.

CONTENTS

PUBLISHED MONTHLY BY THE
National Association for the Advancement of Colored People
AT TWENTY VESEY STREET NEW YORK CITY

ONE DOLLAR A YEAR TEN CENTS A COPY

The first issue of *The Crisis,* the monthly magazine for the NAACP that was first edited by W.E.B. DuBois and made its debut in 1910. DuBois would publish many articles in his lifetime debating the future of black education and the struggle for equality.

training of the college is the development of power, the training of a self whose balanced assertation will mean as much as possible for the great ends of civilization. . . . We must give to our youth a training designed above all to make them men of power, of thought, of trained and cultivated taste; men who know whither civilization is tending and what it means."

The black colleges and universities that DuBois envisioned were modeled on white liberal arts schools. However, DuBois believed black schools were better suited to teach black students, and that a community which supported its students and gave them a sense of heritage could not be found in white schools:

> What is needed then . . . is the College-Bred Community; for no matter how far the college may fail in individual cases, it is, after all, the center where knowledge of the past connects with the ideal of the future.
>
> But, given a group or community which does not know the message of the past and does not have within its own number, the men who can feel it, and is separated from contact with outside groups who can teach it—given such a community and you have a desperate situation.

A few months before he died in 1965, DuBois was interviewed for *The Atlantic Monthly*. He spoke at length about Washington, his admiration for the seminal black leader and his disappointment with his compromises. As DuBois saw it, the South after the Civil War was a society torn apart, with many factions and ideologies struggling for prominence. It was important for black Southerners to force their way into that dialogue, and not accept the lowly status that many white Southerners wanted to confer on them.

DuBois attributed Washington's beliefs to "a certain idealism . . . born out of present reality." By the dawn of the Civil Rights movement, in the 1950s, Washington's views were falling out of favor. A century of segregation, Jim Crow laws, and

disenfranchisement had soured many blacks to the accommo-
dating philosophies of Washington. In addition, an increasing
number of blacks colleges and universities were abandoning their
industrial and normal schools in favor of a liberal arts education.
Over the next two decades, black schools and universities would
undergo dramatic changes as they, like Washington, became
shaped by a present reality.

This photograph shows students of the Whittier School studying plants in 1899. In a survey of black graduates in the 1930s, 21 percent had parents who had at least an eighth-grade education. However, equality in education was still far from reality.

4

Struggle and Acceptance

In the decades between World War I and the Civil Rights era, black colleges and universities became an accepted part of American education. This did not come easily. Black Americans were still beset by poverty and segregation. Black students did not have the same opportunities and resources as most white students, and there were no federal guidelines for black schools. Still, an increasing number of black Americans were receiving at least a basic education. In a survey of black graduates in the 1930s, 21 percent had parents who had received up to an eighth grade education and 14 percent had parents who graduated from college.

The crucial role black colleges and universities played in higher education did not go unnoticed by white Americans. Before the mid-century, the federal government and philanthropy groups had undertaken a series of comprehensive surveys to determine the health of black colleges and universities and document their considerable growth.

The attention from these surveys brought an unprecedented funding to black colleges and universities, which often struggled tremendously to find resources, and nominal acceptance by white educational societies. But the attention was not without a downside. The government surveys continued to advocate industrial education for blacks, even as it became apparent that the most successful black colleges and universities offered a liberal arts curriculum. Money from philanthropic organizations was often designated for the industrial arts over medical or law programs. While the outlook for black colleges and universities was bright, they still existed in a society with highly mixed views about black education.

When Washington and DuBois conducted their public debates over the direction of black higher education, little research had been conducted on black schools that would support or disprove their theories. Black colleges and universities had no reputable indication as to whether or not they were successful. Organizations for accrediting colleges, such as the Southern Association of Colleges and Schools, were not open to black schools. Between 1890 and 1947, various groups undertook studies of black schools. W.E.B. DuBois, who led two surveys, examined whether liberals arts existed in black schools. The Office of Education questioned whether black schools met the federal definition of industrial education. The philanthropic foundations and northern industrialists examined the state of black schools to determine how they should be funded.

At the time the surveys were conducted, widespread disparity existed in black colleges and universities. Some schools offered the same curriculum found in elementary and secondary schools. At Howard University in Washington, D.C., however, a curriculum from 1868-69 required students to be familiar with "two books of *Caesar*, six orations of Cicero, the *Bucolics*, the *Georgics*, six books of Virgil's *Aeneid* . . . and the first two books of Homer's *Iliad*" as a prerequisite for admission. There was much uncertainty about the significance of degrees awarded by the schools. Did a college degree in Arkansas mean the same as one issued in Washington, D.C., or Pennsylvania? The seven major studies undertaken before *Brown v. Board of Education* ended segregation in schools in 1954 attempted to answer these questions. W.E.B. DuBois conducted the first major surveys of black colleges and universities. They were small in scope, covering the economic background and the quality of courses at black schools. DuBois found small enrollments at most black colleges and, consistent with his own philosophy, recommended that the curriculum follow the liberal arts model.

The Phelps-Stokes Report in 1932 proved to be more in-depth. The report was commissioned by the Phelps-Stokes Fund, a foundation established to support education. The report "strongly endorsed industrial education and calling for coop-eration between the races in the implementation of black higher education." Although the report stressed the importance of industrial education over a liberal arts curriculum, it was progressive for its time in that it acknowledged that black higher education could no longer be ignored. The report advocated improved funding from local governments to black colleges and recommended equal pay for black and white teachers. Recognizing the importance of black colleges, the Phelps-Stokes Report recommended that white Southern governments form a closer association with the schools. This had mixed implications for black colleges and universities. While all would welcome eliminating inequity, a stronger government role could possibly detract from the autonomy black schools enjoyed.

Between 1916 and 1942, the federal government conducted four surveys of black colleges and universities. After the Morrill Land-Grant Act of 1890, the government paid little attention to black colleges and universities. Simply documenting the existence of these schools greatly expanded federal awareness of them. The 1916 report prepared extensive documentation on all black colleges and universities, their names, administration, student enrollments, evaluation of future plans, and recommendations for each school. Not unlike the Phelps report, the recommendations focused on increased teacher training and encouraged agricultural education while advising private colleges to drop liberal arts offerings such as foreign languages. A survey the next year examined only black agricultural and mechanical colleges. The report revealed the majority of schools offered distinctly non-college courses such as sewing, cooking, and laundering classes in addition to agricultural and carpentry courses. A progress report in 1928 reexamined all of the schools from the 1916 report. This federal survey affirmed the 1916 recommendations regarding agricultural education. By 1935, over 80 percent of land-grant colleges reported that they had strengthened their agricultural and mechanical programs.

The final survey, conducted by the federal Office of Education in 1942, documented the disparate levels of education provided by black schools. The report "revealed that all of the colleges in the study provided general education, advanced education, and professional and technical education." Although select black schools such as Fisk University and Morehouse and Spelman colleges were considered on par with white universities, most were considered below average. Overall, black colleges "were reported to be making significant changes that reflected faculty opinion and student needs," although the report did not specify those needs. This period of redefinition for black schools would continue throughout the next two decades as students and faculty demanded a larger voice in their schools.

The government reports deemed many black colleges and universities to be substandard compared to the majority of white institutions. However, black higher education was clearly evolving. By 1930, most black schools were colleges in the traditional sense, having dropped their non-college courses and requiring students to have high school diplomas. Between 1914 and 1936, medical degrees accounted for the largest percentage of professional degrees earned by black students.

Despite the reluctance of white researchers to acknowledge the

In the early 1900s, reports compared the quality of black and white schools. These found that the majority of black schools offered such courses as sewing, cooking, and laundering—and most offered education that was not on par with white schools. By the 1930s, most schools had dropped such courses.

value of a liberal arts education for blacks, the reports succeeded in shining a light on the spirit and determination of black schools. By encouraging additional teacher training, improved facilities, and increased funding, these reports acknowledged the value of black colleges and universities. While the reports advocated Booker T. Washington's philosophies, a liberal arts curriculum was evident at many of the surveyed colleges. This suggested that black educators did not subscribe to acquiescence and limited expectations advocated by white researchers. In a time where black inferiority was widely accepted, the existence of a liberal arts education that emphasized math, science, foreign language, and literature indicated "an unwillingness to accept black inferiority as a standard for black higher education." Moreover, in the eyes of the black community, schools such as Fisk, Morehouse, and Spelman had more prestige than industrial schools.

By World War II, black involvement in higher education had become much more visible. In the 1920s, the Southern Association of Colleges and Schools began working with black schools in "conducting surveys, establishing academic rankings, upgrading college programs and formalizing accreditation procedures." In 1931, the American Medical Association approved a petition from 31 black colleges to provide pre-med courses. Black colleges achieved "the scrutiny of the scholar" when the *Journal of Negro Education* began publishing in 1932.

Colleges and universities that wanted to improve their facilities and academic programs often faced an uphill battle. At the beginning of the 20th century, the land-grant colleges were largely funded by church groups and personal donations. Black colleges rarely received the state funding ascribed to white schools. Financial crisis was often and acute. A survey of black schools noted, "no type of education is so eagerly sought by the colored people as college education. Yet no educational institutions for colored people are so poorly equipped . . . as the majority of those claiming to give college education."

Because of scant resources, black schools in the first part of the 20th century built their college programs slowly. Many provided an elementary or secondary education. In 1916, a survey of 653 black schools found that just 2,641 students out of a population of nearly 93,000 were considered college students.

Yet students flocked to black campuses for their college education. In 1953, for instance, over 37,000 students were enrolled in 33 public four-year colleges. As their campuses swelled, "it was necessary for those in charge of the schools to carry on a constant campaign for funds. Many presidents and principals spent the greater part of their time soliciting funds." Unique sources of fund-raising emerged. The Fisk Jubilee Singers "raised large sums of money in the early history of Fisk University" through their singing talents. In fact, "many schools kept quartettes or musical bodies of some kind on the road to sing their way into the hearts of Northern philanthropy and thus induce a benevolent attitude toward the particular school represented."

Other schools faced their hardships by consolidating with nearby black colleges or universities or sharing resources. In 1930, New Orleans had three black colleges: Straight University, New Orleans University, and Xavier College. Straight and New Orleans shared essentially the same mission and goals. In order to achieve true university status, the two schools voted to consolidate into Dillard University. Atlanta's handful of black colleges—Clark University, Morehouse College and Spelman College, Atlanta University, and Morris Brown University—also shared a similar purpose, but "none had any distinctive function or activity that could not be performed by any one of the remainder." In 1929, Atlanta, Morehouse, and Spelman reached an agreement in which Atlanta would continue as a graduate school while Morehouse and Spelman (both single-sex schools) would continue as undergraduate schools.

Consolidation was not an option most schools chose to pursue. Enrollment at public universities had outpaced private colleges by the 1950s but state funding did not suffice. For help, financially strapped schools relied on a group of philanthropic organizations that emerged between 1866 and 1916. Unlike the older missionary groups that had served black schools, the new donors were usually based in the North and were secular. The most prominent philanthropy groups were the Rockefeller Foundation, the General Education Board, the Southern Education Board, the Julius Rosenwall Fund, the Carnegie Foundation, and the Phelps-Stokes Fund. The General Education Board, founded by John D. Rockefeller, gave $63 million to black education until 1960, most of it to black schools. The Julius Rosenwall Fund provided aid in the areas of black education, health and medical services, and fellowships. The Phelps-Stokes Fund contributed to black colleges and universities, and sponsored surveys of black

JUBILEE SINGERS

MAGGIE PORTER. E. W. WATKINS. H. D. ALEXANDER. F. J. LOUDIN. THOMAS RUTLING.
JENNIE JACKSON. MABEL LEWIS. ELLA SHEPPARD. MAGGIE CARNES. AMERICA W. ROBINSON.

The Jubilee Singers were students from Fisk University who would tour to raise money for their school. They even performed at the invitation of Queen Victoria of England.

schools. White Southerners were initially dismayed at money being dedicated to improve black education. Groups such as the General Education Fund, however, assured whites that the stress of the aid would be placed "on industrial, rather than collegiate and professional training for blacks."

Such philanthropy, grounded in notions of black inferiority, clearly was not ideal for black colleges and universities. In addition, when the Great Depression and then World War II struck, already-thin resources were further eroded. In the early 1940s, Frederick D. Patterson, the third president of the Tuskegee Institute, suggested that black private colleges pool their resources and "make a united appeal to the national consciousness." The result was the United Negro College Fund, which launched its first campaign in 1944 with the slogan, "A mind is a terrible thing to waste." In its first year, the Fund raised $765,000, an amount three times larger than the amount raised by the 27 member colleges in previous years.

By the mid-20th century, clearly more blacks sought a college education. Black soldiers returning from World War II were given aid for college as part of the GI Bill. Black illiteracy was disappearing, and increasing numbers of black families sent their children to college. Black colleges and universities no longer had to fight to exist. Instead, they fought for better funding and equal rights, a battle that would be carried to the Supreme Court in 1954, resulting in a decision that changed black colleges and universities and American education forever.

THE LITTLE ROCK NINE

Gloria Ray · Terrance Roberts · Melba Patillo · Elizabeth Eckford · Ernest Green · MinniJean Brown · Jefferson Thomas · Carlotta Walls · Thelma Mothershed

The "Little Rock Nine" were students who were barred from entering high school by the National Guard and a white mob. Desegregation was a painful process that was spearheaded by the *Brown v. Board of Education* decision. It also led to a "brain drain" from segregated black schools.

5

A New Era For Black Schools

The early history of black colleges and universities encapsulates the struggle of black Americans to achieve education and equality. Students and faculty endured battles ranging from neglect to outright hostility simply because they were black and wanted to be educated. After several decades, the threat of segregated black education diminished for white Americans. The federal government undertook several surveys that recommended stronger black schools. Funding was often a tremendous struggle for black colleges and universities, and white philanthropists began investing heavily in the schools. After World War II, returning servicemen—including black soldiers—received education allowances as part of the GI Bill of Rights.

Still, racism was persistent, and blacks and whites remained highly segregated. Blacks and whites rode in different sections of buses, used separate water fountains and received separate educations. A series of lawsuits challenged the notion of a separate but equal education. Between 1935 and 1954, the National Association for the Advancement of Colored People (NAACP) brought five lawsuits to the U.S. Supreme Court challenging the lack of equal educational opportunity. These cases laid the groundwork for the Supreme Court's historical 1954 decision in *Brown v. Board of Education* that declared segregated schools to be unconstitutional.

The decision was a major turning point for black colleges and universities. Over the next three decades, there was an exodus from black institutions to white colleges and universities. The continued relevance of black schools in a post-segregation era turned into a matter of heated debate. Black colleges and universities continued to face severe budget crises due to dropping enrollments, despite a number of laws that increased federal aid to historically black colleges and universities. Legal battles over segregation continued into the 1990s as well, as states attempted to comply with desegregation laws. Would desegregation mean eliminating black schools, or merging black and white colleges and universities? Black leaders argued that black schools should not bear the burden of desegregation.

In the 1990s, enrollment at black schools began an upward trend. This can be attributed to several reasons. A number of studies indicated that black students felt a sense of security on black campuses that they did not feel at predominately white schools. In addition, a mentoring relationship with faculty gave students a deepened sense of investment in their studies. Although test scores for students on black and white campuses were comparable, black students seemed to fare better psychologically overall at black schools. Another factor was the political and social upheaval of the 1960s. Black colleges and universities became more responsive to the needs of students, such as hiring black faculty and developing doctoral programs. Opportunities increased for the brightest black students as well as those who required remedial classes and close mentoring.

Black colleges and universities were acutely aware that economic disadvantages still plagued many black communities. College-age students did not necessarily possess the skills gauged by the Scholastic Aptitude Tests (SATs), but black educators recognized that remedial classes and nurturing could turn around an under-achieving student. Outreach and service projects off-campus also connected students to their surrounding communities while fostering local interest and ties to the school. The tradition of exclusivity found in the oldest white schools was not an option when black schools opened. A century later, inclusiveness is still a hallmark of black education. Many of the brightest black leaders and artists emerged from historically black colleges and universities. Martin Luther King, Jr., and Julian Bond, head of the NAACP, attended Morehouse College. Thurgood Marshall graduated from Lincoln University. Ralph Bunche, the first black Nobel Prize winner, and Toni Morrison, the Pulitzer Prize-winning author, both attended Howard University. Writers and artists Langston Hughes, Nikki Giovanni, Ralph Ellison, Zora Neale Hurston, and Spike Lee all attended black colleges.

SEPARATE BUT UNEQUAL

Beginning in the 1930s, a handful of legal cases chipped away at the inequality inherent in segregated education. The U.S. Supreme Court recognized that Southern states generally neglected the "equal" part of the "separate but equal" doctrine. Black schools at all levels in the South were found to be generally "admittedly inferior." In two cases, the Court ruled that without equal educational opportunities, Missouri and Oklahoma must admit black students to their all-white law schools. In a case brought against the University of Maryland, the Court ruled that states could not force black students to attend out-of-state colleges when the states had failed to integrate their own schools.

In the early 1950s, the NAACP adopted a strategy intent on

"securing a Court ruling on the legality of segregation itself." Under the NAACP's guidance, black parents in several states brought lawsuits against state boards of education. The lawsuits argued that segregated schools violated the 14th Amendment, which provided for equal protection under the law. The case that became *Brown v. Board of Education of Topeka et al.* consolidated lawsuits from parents in Delaware, Washington, D.C., South Carolina, and Virginia.

The lead lawyer for the plaintiffs was Thurgood Marshall, a graduate of Lincoln University and future Supreme Court justice. The NAACP's strategy was to include "states in the South, a border state, a state where slavery had never existed, and the District of Columbia. In these jurisdictions, segregated education has been provided for in state constitutions . . . or had been made an option." By trying to close potential loopholes, the NAACP hoped that the Supreme Court's decision would apply to all states. Although the lawsuit was brought on behalf of elementary school-age children, a change in the separate but equal doctrine would apply to all levels of education, black and white. On May 17, 1954, Supreme Court Chief Justice Earl Warren issued the court's unanimous decision, writing, "Does segregation of children in public schools solely on the basis of race, even though the physical facilities and other 'tangible' factors be equal, deprive the children of the minority group of equal educational opportunities? We believe that it does. We conclude that in the field of education the doctrine of 'separate but equal' has no place."

With their ruling, the Supreme Court ended any legal basis for segregated education in the United States. Black students could no longer be barred from attending the school of their choice. Reaction to the historical decision in the black community was "a combination of exultation and concern. Their exultation arose from their beliefs that the decision was the right and moral thing to do; that it validated the constitutional rights of black American to pursue opportunities outside racial caste lines."

George E. C. Hayes, Thurgood Marshall, and James M. Nabrit were the lawyers who led the legal battle that ended when the Supreme Court declared segregation to be unconstitutional, based on the 14th Amendment.

At the same time, the black community organized "to apply political pressure to make sure, on the one hand, that the new law was enforced and, on the other, that enforcement did not result in a similar system of discrimination." Two years before *Brown*, the president of Morgan State College in Maryland "pointed out that for most of the black colleges integration would mean participation in state systems reorganized to offer services to the majority. The danger was . . . that services designed specifically for black students would disappear and existing patterns of discrimination could be perpetuated under the guise of equality."

Just as the Emancipation Proclamation formally ended slavery but not racism, *Brown* could not immediately undo cultural notions of black inferiority. The decade following the Supreme Court's decision was "marked by massive Southern resistance in the form of demurrers, stalling and physical force." Blacks countered this resistance with marches and protests, and eventually the government compelled Southern schools to desegregate with the use of the National Guard. Three years after the Supreme Court's decision, just 2,400 black students had enrolled in Southern white universities. That number mushroomed to 17,000 in the next seven years. By contrast, in 1953, approximately 45,000 to 50,000 black students attended Northern colleges and universities. Two decades before, W.E.B. DuBois summed up the contradictions evoked by desegregation:

> There is no magic, either in mixed schools or in segregated schools. A mixed school with poor and unsympathetic teachers, with hostile public opinion, and no teaching of truth concerning black folk is bad. A segregated school with ignorant placeholders, inadequate equipment, poor salaries, and wretched housing is equally bad. . . . The mixed school is the broader, more natural basis for the education of all youth. It gives wider contacts; it inspires greater contacts. . . . But other things seldom are equal, and in that case, Sympathy, Knowledge, and the Truth outweigh all that the mixed school can offer.

DuBois' view of desegregated schools was decidedly pessimistic. Following *Brown*, black educators echoed his rhetoric to varying degrees. Benjamin Mays, a former president of the United Negro College Fund, argued that desegregation should not "create an inferiority complex in Negroes or a superiority complex in whites." However, over the next two decades, black students took their chances and flocked to white campuses. This left black schools in the unusual position of competing with white schools for black students. Black colleges and universities were not just assailed by the exodus from their campuses; students who continued to attend black schools pressed for reform throughout the 1960s and '70s.

Despite concern about how desegregation would impact black colleges and universities, the Civil Rights era had many benefits for black schools. Black colleges could now apply for federal funding to improve their facilities and programs, and federal financial aid opened up to black students. The government made two important contributions to the health of black colleges and universities with the Civil Rights Act of 1964 and the Higher Education Act of 1965. In an echo of the Morrill Land-Grant Act of 1890, the Civil Rights Act prohibited the use of federal funds in segregated colleges. White schools had to sign a statement of compliance in order to receive the aid. The Higher Education Act of 1965 also targeted black colleges and universities for assistance. Title VI required states with dual systems of segregation to dismantle. Under Title III of the act, government funds were reserved for "developing institutions," as well as "faculty and curriculum development programs, exchanges of faculty and students between colleges, student services, and improvements in administrative structures."

Although black schools were not specifically mentioned, because of their financial struggles, most were eligible for assistance under Title III. In this way, the act demonstrated the federal government's commitment to the survival of historically black colleges and universities. The act also provided grants to financially needy students, who were often black. The lasting effect of the Higher Education Act was that "it helped reduce the extent to which poverty limited the opportunity of students to pursue a college education." The effect on black campuses was profound. Even as students left to attend white colleges, the number of degrees awarded by HBCUs increased from 13,000 in 1954 or 32,000 in 1974.

BLACK STUDENTS AND THE CIVIL RIGHTS ERA

The burgeoning civil rights movement, led by Martin Luther King, Jr., and the efforts of black students to desegregate schools, radicalized black college campuses in the 1960s and '70s. In the 1950s, it was often the graduates of black colleges and universities who led the fight against segregation. It was during King's studies at Morehouse that he was first introduced to the idea of civil disobedience. He recalled learning how to think critically about race: "There was a free atmosphere at Morehouse, and it was there I had my first frank discussion on race. . . . [The professors] encouraged us in a positive quest for a solution to racial ills. I realized that nobody there was afraid." Picking up King's gauntlet, it was the students on black campuses who played leading roles in the drive toward civil rights during the 1960s.

The era of college sit-ins, in fact, began in 1960 with four students from North Carolina Agricultural and Technical College, a black school. When the students were denied service at an all-white lunch counter in Greensboro, they refused to leave until the diner closed. The next day, they returned and sat at the counter for the entire day. Word of the students' sit-in spread, and within days, students from four black colleges in North Carolina took similar action. Media coverage of the sit-ins depicted "students peacefully requesting service in lunch counters, being physically abused by segregationists, and carted off to jail by the police." On black campuses, college presidents worried about funding usually did not publicly support sit-ins, but "they seldom failed to make adjustments when scheduled campus activities conflicted with the protests."

James Meredith was the first black student to attend the University of Mississippi. His mere attendance required military protection—which was similar to the experience of other black students who were among the first to step onto white campuses.

The Civil Rights movement politicized a new generation of black students. Interest in black culture exploded in the 1960s. In 1966, black leader Stokely Carmichael used the term "black power" at the Freedom March rally led by James Meredith, the first black student to attend the University of Mississippi. The phrase embodied the prevailing mood of empowerment and action that swept black colleges and universities. Criticism turned inward, and black schools came under much criticism from students and faculty. One teacher from Tougaloo College, a small private school in Mississippi, recalled:

> Our students were very idealistic [in the '60s]. Many were active in the Civil Rights Movement and all felt the world could be greatly improved. They believed that the economically deprived and the socially outcast would prevail, and they challenged any threat to their ideals. Then the militancy which had been directed to the controlling white society outside the gates began to turn inward. Students began to challenge the authority of the college administration and faculty.

Students questioned whether administrations were committed to change or the status quo. They wanted facilities and resources to be equal to white colleges and universities while remaining sensitive to the black experience. Two of the predominant issues for black students in the 1960s and '70s were "the expansion of curriculum to include a wider range of professional studies [and] increased attention to black history and culture within the curriculum."

Until the 1960s, the administration at black colleges was often predominately white. Students demanded that more black faculty be hired and that students share a greater voice in the affairs of the college. On black campuses throughout the country, students criticized what they viewed as a conservative administration. For much of their history, black schools had struggled for resources and made do with inadequate facilities. Graduates could expect limited entry into the white career world. Starting in the 1960s, laws and shifting cultural attitudes allowed an increasing number of black students into white-collar professions. With the Higher Education Act and the Civil Rights Act, black schools had a wider variety of financial opportunities.

Recognizing this shift in society, students on black campuses pushed their administration for greater change. Toward the end of the decade, black studies began to develop as an academic program at a handful of colleges—most of them white universities like Cornell and Yale. Black studies were slower to take root at black schools. In the book *Stand and Prosper,* Henry Drewry and Humphrey Doermann write that black schools "would prove more conservative than their harder-pressed white counterparts— and, as ever, they would have more immediate issues of survival to consider."

Because the academic programs of many black schools were slow to adjust to the fiery times, students decried what they called the "plantation milieu" and "missionary mentality" of black colleges and universities. The protests sometimes turned ugly or violent. At Texas Southern University, a policeman was killed and students fired upon during a protest of the school's administration. At Howard University, students hung an effigy of the school's administration and held repeated sit-ins and boycotts until the president of the school, who was black, resigned.

Clearly black colleges and universities had a new student body that would not be ignored. An article in a 1963 *Negro Digest* called "for a basic re-examination of our college curricula and a questioning of the continuing exclusive emphasis upon traditionalism. . . . We must be alert to the vastly increasing categories of skills . . . which will be available to the graduates of the 1960s, little dreamed of a few years ago."

Ten years later, the goals were the same, but the ideals were more radical. A 1973 issue of the *Journal of Black Studies* defined the new role for black colleges and universities. Black schools are "confronted with the difficult task of transforming a middle-class liberal arts institution . . . into a broad-ranging, community-oriented, socially inclusive institution." It would not be enough to train black medical students, for example. Black colleges

A grim scene at Texas Southern University following a riot in 1967. College campuses were the scenes of protests that often turned violent in the 1960s. Desegregation would endure growing pains for years to come.

and universities should provide "premedical science courses as viewed from a black perspective, public health issues from the standpoint of the need of the black community, and so on."

COURT CASES AFTER *BROWN*

Throughout the 1970s and '80s, several lawsuits further defined the meaning and scope of desegregation. Title VI, which ordered states to dismantle dual systems of higher education, was problematic as it "did not identify what was meant by discrimination based on race or national origin." In 1969, the Office of Civil Rights reviewed the results of desegregation and determined that in 10 states, "black schools were still nearly all black, and historically white schools were still virtually all white." The Department of Health, Education, and Welfare (HEW) asked the states to submit plans of desegregation. Five refused and the other five states submitted plans considered unacceptable. In 1970, the NAACP filed a lawsuit against HEW charging the department with failing to adequately oversee desegregation. Three years later, a U.S. District Court ruled that the states had violated the Civil Rights Act and compelled HEW to enforce desegregation.

Civil rights groups praised the decision. Black colleges and universities adopted a more critical stance. A consortium of black educators argued to the court that, historically, black colleges had always opened admissions to all races and creeds. They had not practiced segregation and therefore should not bear the burden of desegregation. The argument was successful. The court issued a decision honoring the unique role of historically black colleges and universities and ordered the states to take into account "the real danger that desegregation will diminish higher education opportunities."

The process of desegregating white schools while maintaining the integrity of historically black schools was often a delicate balancing act of competing interests. In 1975, a group of black Mississippians filed a lawsuit against the state arguing that the Title VI had not been enforced. The case, *Ayers v. Fordice*, traveled through the legal system for nearly 20 years before the U.S. Supreme Court issued its decision. The court's ruling had potentially far-reaching implications for black colleges. They rejected the state of Mississippi's view that adopting a race-neutral policy would be sufficient to dismantle desegregation. The court ruled that "the state would have to justify or eliminate any policies that 'substantially restrict a

person's choice' of institution or 'contribute to the racial iden-
tifiability of the eight public universities.'" The court also failed
to single out historically black schools for special protection.

While *Fordice* did not render black schools unconstitutional in
and of themselves, the court did identify them as remnants of
segregation. Closings and mergers were suggested as possible
solutions. The court also noted that Mississippi's black and white
colleges and universities shared duplicate programs, which
violated the separate but equal doctrine. The *Fordice* decision
has been called "the most important Supreme Court ruling
affecting the education of blacks since [*Brown*]." After the ruling,
Mississippi raised entrance requirements at its three public black
universities, resulting in an enrollment decline at all three—
including a 20 percent drop at Mississippi Valley State University.
While no HBCU has yet closed as result of *Fordice*, it has
placed historically black schools in a vulnerable position
where the Supreme Court considers them, at least, to be a vestige
of segregation.

As the courts untangled the definition of desegregation,
the federal government continued its financial support of
historically black colleges and universities. When Congress
reauthorized the Higher Education Act in 1986, it allocated
$100 million exclusively for historically black colleges. Three
years later, President George H. W. Bush issued an executive
order intending to strengthen the capacity of black colleges and
universities to provide quality education.

The future of historically black colleges and universities does
not lie solely with the courts and federal government. The past
three decades have seen great shifts in student population—first
an exodus to white schools, and, in the past decade, a return to
historically black schools. Overall, enrollment rose 21 percent
at HBCUs between 1976 and 1994, but black enrollment at
predominately white colleges rose 40 percent in the same time
period. In addition, a 1994 report by the federal government
found that enrollment at HBCUs rose 26 percent between 1976

and 1994, but nearly all of that increased occurred between 1986 and 1994. While the numbers of black students attending black colleges has dropped, overall the number of black students attending all colleges has risen substantially, so the drop is less noticeable. And, according to some studies, the rate of attrition for black students at white colleges is much higher than for black students at black schools.

Black schools continue to award a healthy number of degrees and have made great strides into graduate education. In 1999 just 21 percent of all black undergraduates attended historically black colleges and universities, yet HBCUs awarded 28 percent of all degrees awarded to black students. Xavier University in Louisiana sends more students to medical school than any other school in the country. According to a 1999 report, 33 percent of black students continued on to black graduate schools even though only 28 percent of all black students had attended a historically black college or university as undergraduates. At Spelman College, an all-female school in Atlanta, half of the graduating class went on to graduate school. The number of doctorates conferred by HBCUs rose by 223 percent between 1976 and 1994—more than half in the field of education. In 1994, 48 percent of all black undergraduates received their degree in agriculture and natural resources from a historically black college; 45 percent in mathematics, 45 percent in the physical sciences; 40 percent in biological sciences; 38 percent in education and 37 percent in computer sciences. Between 1976 and 1994, enrollment of women at HBCUs rose by 41 percent while enrollment of men rose just nine percent.

The number of white students at historically black schools has also risen dramatically, changing the face of a few black schools. From 1976 to 1994, white enrollment at HBCUs increased by 71 percent. In 1988, historically black colleges and universities comprised roughly two percent of the total college enrollment in the U.S. By 1992, three HBCUs were predominately white, and 10 were more than 20 percent white.

What are some of the reasons black—and white—students continue to choose historically black colleges and universities? Since 1976-77, the number of black colleges and universities offering doctorates had risen from 4 to 15 in 1993-94. This has provided more opportunities for black students who attended predominately white undergraduate institutions and wished to return to black colleges for their advanced degrees.

Cost is also an important factor. According to a survey of student aid in 1989-1990, the average student at an HBCU paid $1,945 in tuition annually compared to $3,309 for a student attending a traditionally white school. A 1999 survey of black schools praised the "affordability of HBCUs, [which] may encourage students, who otherwise either attend a community college or no college at all, to attend a four-year institution." Various studies have shown black students at HBCUs to be more likely to complete their degrees than their black counterparts at traditionally white institutions. Why the turnover? One examination of black schools found close faculty interaction at HBCUs to be an essential factor in the success of black students, which reported that "[Students] experience a greater degree of personal interaction with their professors in many-sided, sustained, and personal relationships beyond the classroom—including counseling sessions and the activities of student organization sponsored by faculty."

The success of graduates of black colleges cannot be denied. A 1986 survey of 2,000 alumni found nearly 90 percent of respondents were professionals in medicine, dentistry, teaching or law. Fifty percent had earned advanced degrees. Evidence suggests that it was the close mentoring at HBCUs that compelled the graduates to succeed. Just six percent felt that their high schools had adequately prepared them for college.

While a handful of black colleges—Howard, Morehouse, and Spelman among them—comprise the "black Ivy League," many black schools are still struggling with financial restraints and enrollment. Some are still poor in terms of physical and teaching facilities. Yet after a century of both indifference and hostility, the unique nature of historically black colleges and universities, their hallmark of multiculturalism and acceptance, have gained respect. One report on black colleges acknowledged this sea change: "White youth could also benefit from adjusting to the different set of race relations and different teaching methods found on an HBCU campus. . . . [Teaching techniques] should be researched . . . to find out why they are apparently so successful with the below-average college student." A student at Hampton University summarized the importance of black colleges: "You can't bottle the nurturing. You can't can the one-on-one dynamics. It made me who I am and what I'm going to be."

Founders Library at Howard University in Washington, D.C. In 1997, Howard's $215 million endowment made it the wealthiest black institution that year.

6

Beloved Communities

Historically black colleges and universities were founded with one mission—to provide an education to those otherwise denied one because of their race. From that common goal, black schools have carved many disparate paths. Because of the largely homogenous population they serve, it would be easy to overlook the considerable differences between historically black colleges and universities. There are the elite schools—Howard University, Spelman College, Morehouse College—with considerable financial resources, and schools that have struggled with debt. There are schools, such as Rust College in Mississippi, where over 90 percent of the student body receives financial aid. There are men's colleges and women's colleges. They are big, small, public, private, four-year, and two-year. All can be said to "have maintained a very close identity with the struggle of blacks for survival, advancement, and equality in American society." This chapter examines the unique character of black colleges and universities.

Howard, Spelman, Morehouse, and Hampton University are among the so-called "black Ivy League." This means they attract the best of the nation's black students and have extensive academic offerings. They are also the wealthiest black colleges and universities. In 1997, Howard had a $215 million endowment, making it the wealthiest black institution that year. Spelman was second with $156 million, Hampton was third with $140 million and Morehouse earned $78 million. But compared with Harvard University—which had an $8.8 billion endowment in 1997—the resources of most historically black colleges and universities are scant. Even the wealthiest black schools struggle, Howard President H. Patrick Swygert pointed out: "Some folks may say, 'Howard's OK. We don't have to help them.' . . . But context is important. Again, it's $200 million for Howard and $5 billion for Yale." In the mid-1990s, Swygert consolidated several of Howard's colleges as a cost-cutting measure.

In 1997, the smallest endowment for a black school was $1.7 million. But the wealthiest black schools do attract top faculty and students and can afford to expand their facilities and update their programs more easily than the majority of black schools. They have the ability to compete for federal research dollars—"research" institutions are generally more acclaimed than "teaching" institutions. Despite this, between 1980-1990, just one percent of all federal research dollars for education went to HBCUs.

Some of the "black Ivy League" schools have flourished since their inception. Tuskegee University, the richest black school when Booker T. Washington headed it, is still among the top 12. Howard, which opened in 1867 with four students, had 97 by the end of its first term. Within seven years the Washington, D.C., university had 11 departments, including law and medical schools and a seminary. Twenty years before southern black colleges were considered for accreditation, Spelman College received an "A" rating from the Southern Association of Colleges and Schools in 1932. Both schools have been the beneficiaries of large endowments that propelled them to the top ranks of black colleges. Spelman, for instance, received $20 million from comedian Bill Cosby and his wife, the single largest donation to a historically black college or university.

There are three single-sex historically black colleges and universities: Morehouse (men's) and Spelman and Bennett College in North Carolina (women's). Each cultivates a tradition and deep sense of pride in its students. At Bennett it is known as the "Bennett Ideal." The school enforced a ladylike dress code, including hats, purses, and white gloves. "They were trying to make classy people out of us," recalled one graduate. Today's students have fewer restrictions, but they are still "taught how to act, what to wear, that ladies don't walk on grass, that they don't chew gum in public," according to one student. The sense of self-worth and pride cultivated in Bennett students, once known as "Bennett belles," has a long history. In the 1930s students picketed local movie theaters because they showed degrading images of blacks. The single-sex environment is important, educators at the Spelman and Bennett say, because sexism erodes self-esteem as much as racism. One Spelman administrator contended, "As a woman's institution, we are successful because we say that there are no limitation. You can only limit yourself here. . . . We want you to assume responsibility. We want you to take care of your sisters. That is a constant refrain on campus."

At Morehouse, the sense of brotherhood and excellence has been termed "The Morehouse Mystique." In an issue of *Black Issues in Higher Education*, a Morehouse student explained: "When I first came here I was timid and didn't have much confidence. . . . At Morehouse, you are surrounded by very intelligent 'brothers,' and that forces you to compete on a higher level." Another student raised in an Atlanta housing project turned down a Harvard scholarship to attend Morehouse. The student said he felt Morehouse's reputation for nurturing to be as important as its academic program: "I knew that if I could

Morehouse College circa 1970. According to Morehouse's statistics, the school turns out five percent of all black doctors and dentists—a significant amount, considering such fields are underrepresented by blacks.

make it to this institution it would help me. Then we would each other."

One criticism leveled at elite schools such as Spelman and Morehouse is that they don't share a commitment to teaching all black students. The schools do, however, offer programs that other black schools do not, in fields still largely closed to blacks. According to Morehouse statistics, the college produces five percent of all black dentists and doctors, and 14 alumni have become presidents of colleges and universities. Spelman developed a science program in the 1970s when less than two percent of the total population of U.S. scientists was black. In 1973, the National Science Foundation reported that only eight percent of black students chose science majors.

Spelman began in 1881 with the purpose to teach freed slaves how to read the Bible and "write well enough to send letters to their families in the North." Over a century later, Spelman has greatly expanded and refined its mission. A student described her sense of the school: "[A] Spelman woman is trying to get somewhere in life. . . . There is a certain responsibility as a college student in America. Not in jail. Not a so-called welfare queen. It's not easy being here." In the early 1970s, the Spelman science program consisted of "dull and dark" science building erected in 1925, poor laboratory facilities and equipment, and an unexceptional curriculum. The student population had little exposure to the problem-solving skills and scientific skills that would encourage them to pursue a science degree. With a decreasing number of Spelman students choosing a science major, the natural sciences department began a five-year over-haul of the program. The plan included an eight-week summer program for entering freshmen who chose math or science as their major; a counseling program specifically for science majors; tutoring in math, chemistry, and biology; and sessions on test-taking techniques. Within four years, the number of majors in the natural sciences had more than doubled. By the late 1990s, 38 percent of Spelman students were choosing the natural sciences—chemistry, biology, math, and engineering—as their major.

After Spelman overhauled its science department, the summer program was considered the most successful feature of the plan. Recognizing the financial constraints of many Spelman students, the college paid a stipend to students to compensate for the loss of summer employment. Most black colleges and universities have a significant population that requires financial aid. Unlike Spelman, a good number of historically black colleges are small and underfunded. Many have struggled to stay open or redefined their mission to attract students. With fewer faculty to concentrate on research, small schools usually lack the federal research dollars that schools such as Howard receive. Many of the poorer schools are in rural areas. In the upheaval and loss of student population that followed desegregation, 10 black colleges and universities, including Bishop College in Texas and Simmons University in Kentucky, closed their doors in the '70s and '80s. Some schools lost their accreditation—meaning the quality of school was below an acceptable level.

Leadership often plays a tremendous role in the vitality of a school. In their book, *Stand and Prosper*, authors Henry N. Drewry and Humphrey Doermann contend, "Often the difference between relative success and absolute failure was the leadership of a single figure, a president who stood between existence and collapse." This is true of both thriving and struggling black colleges. The smaller schools that have redeveloped their approach to finding and educating students have benefited from a clear vision, good leadership, and, in some cases, a stroke of financial luck. A 1992 article in *Black Issues of Higher Education* described how the smallest HBCUs prosper despite limited resources: "[They don't] have the mega-million-dollar science facility, the glitzy center for the arts, or the nationally renowned football team that larger schools have. What [they] do have . . . is the will to see to it that no Black student who wants to go to college be turned away."

Allen University in South Carolina had lost its accreditation and was millions of dollars in debt in the mid-1980s. Allen revitalized itself and its surrounding community by offering students in the nearby projects "the start-up money they need to make a down payment on their tuition." By 1992, the school had regained its accreditation and more than doubled its enrollment. Barber-Scotia College in North Carolina employed a similar outreach to its students. One of the former president's explained, "Not all the students who come here are ready for college. . . . We don't turn these students away, we bring them in and work with them."

From its inception, Barber-Scotia has continually redefined its purpose. The school was founded as a seminary in 1867, became Scotia Women's College in 1916, and in 1930, merged with Barber Memorial College in Alabama to become Barber-Scotia. Men were admitted in 1954. One of its first students, Mary McLeod Bethune, later founded another historically black school, Bethune-Cookman College. Within several decades, the school faced serious troubles. By the early 1990s, Barber-Scotia was millions of dollars in debt. From 1988 to 1997, the school went through seven presidents. One of the oldest buildings on campus, Faith Hall, was closed because the school couldn't afford repairs. Students and faculty left in droves.

Most seriously, the Southern Association of Colleges and Schools placed the school on probation. If Barber-Scotia lost their accreditation, they would also lose crucial federal grants and financial aid. The loss of accreditation was often a death knell for colleges. In 1996, Barber-Scotia selected Sammie Potts as its next leader. Potts had previously been at Mary Holmes College, a historically black school in Mississippi. When he arrived at Holmes, the school was over $1 million in debt. Potts identified the elimination of Barber-Scotia's debt as his main priority, a challenging task. "It's difficult when you sit down with someone who thought you were going to close because you were placed on probation. People are always reluctant to become investors when they think you are not going to be around. People always ask the question: 'So, how long are you going to be around?'"

When Potts left the school, the debt was gone, a new learning resources center had opened, and the college was off academic probation. The students and faculty had been pared down to the most dedicated. In 1993, 300 students entered Barber-Scotia as freshmen. Four years later, just 30 members of the

Mary McLeod Bethune, the founder of Bethune-Cookman College in Daytona Beach, Florida. Bethune was a student at Barber-Scotia College in North Carolina. Barber-Scotia, like some other HCBUs, struggled with financial problems.

original group remained. Students and faculty who stayed did so out of loyalty and belief that the school's fortunes could be turned around. Travon Moorer, one of the class of '93, said faculty told him he should leave. Moorer told one of his teachers,

"'I'm here for you. You can give me an opportunity and I am sticking with you.' I've been with the school when it was up and I'll be with it when it's down." Revitalization has not an easy task. The school underwent audits to determine what programs it should keep and which to dismantle. By 1997, the graduating class had reached about 70 students, and Potts said he dreamed of a day when 100 would graduate. A commitment to providing an education to students who might not otherwise have a chance is one that resonated with those who stayed at the Barber-Scotia. One faculty member said, "The key factor for the faculty that stayed was knowing that the college needed to be here for those students."

Between Barber-Scotia and booming institutions like Howard and Spelman are medium-sized schools that lack large endowments but maintain a distinguished tradition and mission. Talladega College in Alabama is such a school. The origins of the school date back to 1865, when a group of former slaves gathered to discuss the possibility of education. Neither Talladega County nor the five surrounding counties had any schools for black children. The newly freed men and women declared "the education of our children and youths as vital to the preservation of our liberties, and true religion as the foundation of all real virtue, and shall use our utmost endeavors to promote these blessings in our common country."

Two years later, the American Missionary Society opened Talladega with one building, four teachers, and 140 students. The original building was constructed with lumber from a dismantled carpenter's shop and an abandoned brick building that was later purchased to stand as a permanent structure. The earliest classes focused on punctuation and articulation. The first principal found students by visiting black churches and asking the congregation to send him the "best specimen of a young man." He promised that the boy would be returned as a teacher for their community. Within the next few years a dormitory for female students and teachers was built, and a theological department established. Like all black colleges, Talladega adapted as a method of survival. Although the school's philosophy was based in the liberal arts, it opened an industrial school "in the least conspicuous corner of this campus" in order to secure funding, which in that era favored industrial education.

By 1890, Talladega offered college courses and within five years had granted its first baccalaureate degrees. From the beginning, Talladega County had firm grassroots ties to the school. In the early 1870s, students from the theological department constructed 25 churches in and around Talladega. Students returned home during summer break to teach local children. The college also donated property to the town of Talladega in 1915 for the purpose of building an elementary school. Talladega's drive and dedication brought it much attention, even from white educational organizations. By 1928 many white Northern schools recognized a Talladega degree even though the Southern Association of Colleges and Secondary Schools refused to accredit black schools. The University of Chicago went so far as to accept Talladega's honors graduates without further examination.

One student who entered Talladega in 1944 said the school was instrumental to building her self-esteem and sense of worth as a black person: "The small college environment encouraged one to be a 'doer' as well as an observer. The atmosphere promoted the 'take what you have and make what you want' approach to life. I found this to be very good for the development of creative thinking." Talladega's success is credited to its strong and visionary leadership. One president who took over in 1908 separated the college program from the secondary school and replaced the college department with a school devoted to the arts and sciences. The next president secured enough grants and funding that by 1932 Talladega was ranked seventh among private black colleges for its endowment.

A year later, the college gambled on its future when it chose Buell Gallagher, a 29-year-old teacher who had never worked at a black school, as its president. The trustees wanted someone to provide a fresh outlook on Talladega's mission. During Gallagher's tenure, Talladega revised its curriculum to include introductory courses in areas such as the humanities, foreign languages, and math. Majors were introduced and each student was required to complete a thesis project for graduation. Another highlight—unusual for it era—was Gallagher's creation of a college council including faculty, students, and administration.

The young president was considered a great success. But Talladega entered into a difficult period in the 1940s when the next president dismantled the school's elementary and secondary schools to the dismay of the local community. The rift between the president and school deepened, and the board of trustees dismissed the entire administration in 1952. The rift reopened in the 1960s when students launched protests for a stronger role in campus politics. A substantial list of demands was presented, covering student social life, security, and even food service. Student marches and sit-ins continued over the Vietnam War, the arrest of two students, and a white professor who was accused of forcefully removing a student from his office. The actions, not atypical of the times, represented the efforts of Talladega students "to eliminate social restrictions and gain greater voice in decision-making."

As black students entered white colleges and universities, Talladega's enrollment depleted. And as racial tension eased in the South, black faculty felt comfortable leaving Talladega's isolated, rural environment for larger cities like Birmingham. Even in tumultuous times, Talladega continued to excel. In 1961 it was ranked 18th in the percentage of all students in the U.S. who received medical degrees. It was among the first black schools to offer a science doctorate, and has tied with Howard University for the highest number of female doctorates produced. Although Talladega was buffeted by enormous change and societal demands throughout the 1970s and '80s, its early history indicates "the importance over a sustained period of time of sound leadership committed to a set of basic, agree-upon goals."

The same could be said about Howard University. One of the wealthiest and most elite of the historically black colleges and universities, Howard had the benefit of being in the nation's capital, the source for all federal funding. Unlike most HBCUs, Howard was established as an act of Congress in 1867. And it is named for Oliver O. Howard, the white man who administered the Freedmen's Bureau.

Howard was initially intended to be a seminary for "training black ministers to help uplift the nearly four million remaining slaves." Unlike many black schools that were formed to teach largely uneducated people and, as a result, taught a more basic curriculum, Howard opened with teaching, medical, law, theological, and agricultural schools. Because of its connection to Oliver Howard, the Freedmen's Bureau was instrumental in providing the fledgling school with facilities. The bureau, which kept offices on the campus, purchased the tract of land the school was built on, and by 1869 had given the school three buildings as gifts.

Howard grew substantially, both academically and physically, and in 1928, was placed in the same category as the black land-grant colleges. This made the school eligible for federal funding under the 1890 Morrill Act, a great boost to the university. The first black president of Howard, Mordecai Johnson, was appointed in 1926, and by his retirement in 1960, the school had 20 new buildings and ten fully accredited schools and colleges. In the decades before desegregated colleges and universities, Howard also produced nearly 50 percent of "the nation's African American doctors, dentists, architects, and engineers, and 96 percent of the nation's lawyers."

The next administration experienced much more turbulent,

Howard University founder Oliver Otis Howard, a former army officer and administrator of the Freedmen's Bureau. Howard was established as an act of Congress in 1867—and being located in Washington, D.C., helped to garner federal funding.

reflecting the societal unrest of the time. Students who wanted a more vocal role at Howard challenged the administration. In 1967, students demonstrated to eliminate compulsory Reserve Officers' Training Corps (ROTC) courses for freshmen and sophomores. Political activism had been banned on campus, and students demanded a pardon for student leaders prosecuted under this rule. The administration denied the request and a class boycott erupted. A year later, distrust between students and the administration deepened. Students staged a sit-in in support of students who were disciplined for destroying an American flag and school property. About 700 students occupied the administration building overnight and prohibited anyone from entering the building. After three days, the school shut down. The administration would not meet the demonstrators' demands—which included the removal of the university president—but the board of trustees did agree to include students and faculty in designing a new curriculum, and to appoint deans and department heads only after consulting faculty. In a victory for students, a new judiciary system would be assigned to handle discipline issues. However, unrest continued, and the following year the College of Medicine led a 22-day boycott and occupation of the office of the president. In the spring of 1969, the president resigned.

Ultimately, the turmoil resolved itself through change and accommodation. "Institutions realized that in order to survive it was necessary to respond to the changes in environment, whether internal or external." A new curriculum emphasized liberal arts and general education courses that exposed students to a greater array of knowledge. This contributed to students feeling as though their Howard degree would make them competitive in the outside world. As the university identified itself as an elite destination for black students, basic academic courses were dropped and such programs as work-study, study abroad, independent study and community service gained precedence. The programs were meant to encourage independence for an increasingly sophisticated and demanding student population. Although Howard encourages its students toward community service, it has chosen to position itself as an elite black institution. Since the 1960s, Howard has gradually raised such admission requirements as SAT scores. The attempt to "eliminate deficiencies and mediocrity" was hoped to improve the school's growing reputation as a research institution.

The challenges black colleges and universities face are immense. One historian commented that black colleges have "occupied a more strategic intermediary position in race relations, and [have] been therefore more of a focus of political pressures and social tension than is commonly expected to be true of educational institutions." The essential element that binds a successful black campus, regardless of size, purpose, and financial health, is unity.

Benjamin Mays, former president of the United Negro College Fund. One of the things Mays felt strongly about was black colleges and universities not only emphasizing famous white writers such as Shakespeare, but black ones such as Langston Hughes.

7

The Future

Black colleges and universities have undertaken a dual mission: to educate the mind while examining and preserving the experience of black people in America. In *The Education of Black People*, W.E.B. DuBois proposed a simple foundation for black colleges and universities, saying, "[T]he university education of black men in the United States must be grounded in the condition and work of those black men."

The universal culture taught in college classrooms must also incorporate "the individual life and individual conditions of living Negroes." Benjamin Mays, former president of the United Negro College Fund, argued that black institutions of higher learning are keepers of black history and tradition, and their role is to impart that to students. Unlike predominately white institutions, the black school has a double role:

They must be as concerned with Shakespeare, Tennyson and Marlowe as the white colleges. But the Negro institutions must give equal emphasis to the writings of Paul Dunbar, Countee Cullen, and Langston Hughes. As much emphasis as white colleges to white sociologists, but equal attention to black sociologists. . . . It is not enough for black colleges to teach their students the economics of capitalism. The graduate of a black college must also understand the problems of the small black capitalist and be able to help him.

Providing a dual education for black students is a continuing challenge for black colleges and universities. The decades following desegregation have been troubled ones for black schools. Several failed to acclimate and closed. According to Drewry and Doermann, financial struggles led schools to "raise tuition more rapidly than they had previously done, and some launched larger and more comprehensive capital fund drives." While black enrollment in college has risen, most of the increase has been on white campuses. In addition, legal challenges to segregation could have a potentially harmful impact on the future of historically black colleges and universities.

In 1967, Vivian Henderson, the president of Clark College, a historically black school, identified several "forces for change" that would test the resiliency and flexibility of black colleges and universities. They included a "move toward elimination of racial dualism" in America and a new wave of black Americans who recognize education as a right and not a privilege, and demand higher standards for their schools as a result. Henderson also mentioned improved educational opportunities, social conflict "between the haves and have nots," and a "galloping technology" that would lead to the development of new careers.

Today's black colleges and universities are facing the same challenges Henderson outlined 30 years ago. How have they risen to the challenge? Statistics show a rise in enrollment at black colleges and universities within the past decade. In addition, a number of surveys have examined the reasons why black colleges are a destination for a growing number of black students, as well as students of other races. Evidence suggests that black students thrive in an environment largely free of racism and one that is culturally sensitive to their experiences. The mentoring relationship with faculty that many black students describe is another crucial factor. There is also the perception that black schools are welcoming of students with poor or undistinguished backgrounds. Despite the financial troubles faced by many black schools, HBCUs continue to offer very low tuitions. Students at HBCUs pay approximately $1,946 in tuition compared to $3,310 for tuition at traditional white schools.

The supportive environment that many studies indicate is key to the success of black schools takes many forms. At Spelman College, for example, "students have their meals in a cafeteria surrounded by oil portraits of outstanding black women, and who are exposed constantly to such visitors to their campus." One survey asked whether instructors included references to blacks in a particular field of study when relevant. At historically black schools, nearly 58 percent of students agreed compared to nearly 21 percent at predominately white schools. Generally, black students at black schools report much more positive experiences than black students at white schools. In one survey, 65 percent of black students on white campuses "experienced racist attitudes," compared to about 27 percent of black students on black campuses with the same experience. Moreover, a number of HBCUs have reported an increase in the number of students transferring from white schools. In 1992, 73 percent of the transfer students at Rust College came from predominately white institutions. Several other schools, including Coppin State University in Maryland, Lincoln University in Missouri and Morris College in South Carolina have reported similar trends.

A study of black students suggested the closely knit dynamic extended beyond the college experience. On black campuses, according to Julian B. Roebuck and Komanduri S. Murty, students tend to perceive each other as "a significant group of students who shared with them a common racial and cultural heritage. They were brothers and sisters on the same campus; potential boyfriends, girl-friends, and mates; fellow members of the fraternities and sororities;

future partners in the black community beyond the campus; members of the future enlightened black leadership seeking justice in a racially segregated society; and future professionals and role models in the black community." Yet, "all were aware of individual differences among themselves, such as personality traits, lifestyles, social class and academic competence."

Wenglinsky also noted, "students attending HBCUs, and black students in particular, are more likely to aspire to a graduate education after college and to obtain a job in one of the professions." A 1996 study found that black students on white campuses were less likely to finish their degrees than students at black schools. Half of the seniors at Spelman, for instance, continue on to graduate study. Xavier University, a Catholic HBCU in New Orleans, has a stunning record of achievement. Xavier is second in the nation for sending its graduates to medical school. Although the average SAT score at Xavier is 825 the school nurtures its students with introductory courses, summer enrichment programs, and peer support. As a result, 93 percent of Xavier students who attend medical school receive their medical degrees.

The success of black students in the sciences has been attributed to dedicated professors willing to work closely in difficult courses. In fact, the leadership and faculty support are widely considered the key to the success of all students at black institutions. One study found "on HBCU campuses, positive black role models are present and readily available on a one-on-one basis. . . . This unique relationship, some feel, is the chief reason for the HBCUs' success." In one survey, the respondents described their teachers as "friendly, accepting, helpful, competent, and empathetic; worthy counselors and mentors; [and] intellectual and moral role models." The respect, students felt, was mutual. They described black faculty as "dot[ing] on them as worthy black students, surrogate children, and an enlightened generation; future professionals and leaders in the black community; future friends, supporters, alumni, and colleagues; and the preservers and carriers of black culture."

Despite this, faculty at black colleges and universities generally

Joseph Meredith—son of James Meredith, the first black student to attend the University of Mississippi—sits beside his daughter at the 2002 commencement ceremonies at the University of Mississippi School of Business, where he received a doctorate degree in business administration.

earn less than faculty at traditionally white schools. In 1994, female faculty at HBCUs earned an average of 14 percent less than female faculty at white schools and male faculty at HBCUs earned 21 percent less than their counterparts at white institutions.

A former faculty member at Bethune-Cookman College in Florida recalled that when students migrated toward white colleges in the 1960s, instructors had to revise their approach and test their flexibility: "Faculty had to become accustomed to extreme variations in the ability and preparation of entering students, and also had to be prepared to teach and reach those students." Another professor from Fisk University described the changes black faculty had to cope with: "'temporary abatements' in faculty and staff salaries; streamlining of all curricula, dropping of some majors, development of cooperative and dual degree programs, and a revamped general education program; greater emphasis on shared university governance; and overhaul of administrative functions." In the 1990s, when Bethune-Cookman's enrollment once again began to increase, it was attributed to the welcoming environment of HBCUs: "Many students returning to our colleges expressed their need for more 'nurturing' than had been received at the majority institutions. . . . HBCUs have been traditionally noted for the kind of atmosphere that allow[s] a student to enter 'where they are' and be nurtured to 'where they should be.'"

Black colleges and universities have approached this challenge in different ways. In their earliest days, black schools admitted students with little or no prior education. Today's black schools have reached out to economically disadvantaged students, and continue to offer remedial classes and flexible admission requirements. Critics have charged that this policy turns black schools into a "paper mill," churning out graduates with vastly different levels of knowledge.

Yet public service for the disenfranchised is considered a hallmark of historically black schools. In an essay on the self-concept of black schools, Gregory Kamerstein writes: "Perhaps the greatest and most distinctive contribution of the black colleges to the American philosophy of higher education has been to emphasize and legitimate public and community service as a major objective of colleges and universities." Service is defined variously as "extension and adult education programs; responsiveness to the needs of the black community . . . training for leadership; faith in democracy; financial aid to promising students who otherwise would have little chance of access to higher education." A number of black schools mention community service in their mission statements. Langston University in Oklahoma, for instance, encourages research "toward solving problems of people in Oklahoma."

Black colleges have also maintained their commitment to open admission, devoting "their energies to creating opportunities rather than constructing rationales for selectivity." Virginia Union University defines their view as "entering qualifications of the students . . . are important, but they are secondary to the qualifications of the graduating student." In 1994, the Department of Housing and Urban Development (HUD) issued grants to 28 historically black colleges to "help revitalize communities around their campuses." Bennett College in North Carolina built an apartment complex and child-care center on the school property. Residents, who were coming off the welfare rolls, received intensive guidance from social workers, a nutritionist, and other faculty. Central State University in Ohio received a HUD grant to renovate 12 dilapidated houses, which is overseen by the schools' Department of Industrial and Technical Education.

The history of historically black colleges and universities has resulted in paradoxical present. Black schools are symbols of a past era when blacks were considered inferior and largely excluded from white society. Yet they evolved into the first truly multicultural American institutions of higher learning. Moreover, black schools have "discarded the notion that higher education is an advantage open only to the rich or socially prestigious." As integrated, socially concerned institutions, they have much to offer American society. Historian Howard Zinn has suggested that rather than dismantle black schools as remnants of segregation, they be viewed as models of 21st century education:

> What is overlooked is that the Negro colleges have one supreme advantage over the others: they are the nearest this country has to a racial microsm of the world outside the United States, a world largely non-white [and] developing and filled with the tensions of bourgeois emulation and radical protest. And with more white students and foreign students entering, Negro universities might become our first massively integrated, truly international educational centers.

1600s The first slaves are brought from Africa to America.

1636 Harvard University, the first college in America, opens.

1798 Eli Whitney invents the cotton gin. The device, which separates cotton fiber from seeds, makes cotton production much quicker and efficient. It also increased the need for slaves on Southern cotton plantations. In 1803, for example, over 20,000 slaves were brought to Georgia and South Carolina to work in the cotton fields.

1826 The first black man receives a degree from an American university, Bowdoin College in Maine.

1830s In response to slave revolts, Southern states enact "black codes," which forbid the instruction of slaves.

1837 The Institute for Colored Youth opens for black students in Philadelphia. Founded by a Quaker, the school is later renamed Cheyney University of Pennsylvania.

1854 Lincoln University opens in Pennsylvania.

1856 Wilberforce University opens in Ohio.

1861 After decades of conflict between North and South, and growing outrage over slavery, the Civil War begins.

1861–70 The American Missionary Society establishes seven black colleges.

1863 President Lincoln issues the Emancipation Proclamation, freeing all slaves.

1862 Congress passes the Morrill Land-Grant Act, which provides federal land to states for the purpose of opening colleges and universities. Only one black college is opened under the act.

1865 The Freedmen's Bureau is organized by the federal government to help the four million newly freed blacks. When the bureau was dissolved in 1872, it had established over 4,200 schools.

1866 Congress passes the 14th Amendment, which gives full citizenship to blacks and guarantees that all laws will apply equally to blacks and whites.

1876 Edward Bouchet is the first black man to receive a Ph.D. in physics, from Yale University.

1888 Tuskegee Institute opens with Booker T. Washington as its head. Washington's view that black schools should provide an industrial education grounded in practical skills would take root in many black colleges and universities.

1890 The Morrill Land-Grant Act is revised so that states that open land-grant colleges must either open their doors to black students or build black schools. The majority choose to build black schools. Between 1870 and 1910, over 100 black colleges and universities are founded. Thesurviving schools are known today as historically black colleges and universities.

1896 In *Plessy v. Ferguson*, the U.S. Supreme Court affirms the right of state governments to operate separate facilities for blacks and whites as long as the facilities were equal. The decision provided the basis for black colleges and universities. The separate but equal doctrine allowed segregation to continue until it was overturned by the Supreme Court in 1954.

1903 W.E.B. DuBois publishes "The Souls of Black Folk." He advocates a liberal arts education as a way to remove the psychological bonds of slavery and produce black leaders. He sharply criticizes Booker T. Washington's philosophy for further oppressing black people.

1916–42 The federal government conducts four surveys of black colleges and universities. They document the state and progress of black schools, and comprise the most comprehensive studies to date. While the surveys advocate increased financial aid and support for black schools, they also recommend an emphasis on industrial education over a liberal arts curriculum.

1921 Sadie Alexander is the first black woman to receive a Ph.D., in economics from the University of Pennsylvania.

1925 Elbert Frank Cox receives his Ph.D. in math from Cornell University. He is the first black in the world to receive a math doctorate.

1930–50s The Supreme Court rules that white colleges and universities in Missouri, Oklahoma, and Maryland must admit black students if there is not a black school that offers the same curriculum.

1931 The American Medical Association approves a petition from 31 black colleges to offer pre-med courses.

1934 Ralph Bunche is the first black man to receive a Ph.D. in political science, from Harvard University.

1944 Congress authorizes the GI Bill of Rights, which provided government aid to servicemen after World War II. The most important provision of the act was educational aid, which paid for four years of college and living expenses. As a result, more black servicemen began attending black colleges and universities.

1944 Strapped for cash, a group of black colleges join forces to launch the United Negro College Fund. The money raised by the fund would be divided among its members. In its first year the fund raised $765,000.

1950s The University of Illinois awards the first Ph.D. in accounting to a black man, named William Campfield.

1954 The Supreme Court overturns segregation with *Brown v. Board of Education.* The court decides that segregation violates the civil rights of black Americans.

1960 Four students from a black college in North Carolina stage a sit-in at a local lunch counter to protest continued segregation, beginning an era of sit-ins and protests throughout college campuses.

1964 Congress passes the Civil Rights Act of 1964. One provision prohibits federal funding to segregated schools.

1965 Congress passes the Higher Education Act of 1965. The government reserves funds for "developing institutions," largely interpreted to mean black colleges and universities. The act also provided grants to financially needy black students. As a result, more blacks are able to attend college.

1967 The prestigious honor society Phi Beta Kappa admits its first black school, Morehouse College.

1970s The NAACP files a lawsuit, known as *Adams v. Richardson,* charging that 10 states have not desegregated their schools. A U.S. District Court eventually rules that when desegregating schools, states must not place an undue burden on black colleges and universities.

1975–92 A lawsuit, known as *Ayers v. Fordice,* filed by a group of Mississippians charging that the Civil Rights Act has not been enforced reaches the Supreme Court in 1992. The court rules that adopting a race-neutral policy is not enough for states to prove they have desegregated their schools. While not specifically mentioning historically black schools, the court decides that the state must justify or eliminate any school that is racially identifiable. The Clinton administration announces it will not support the closing of historically black schools to achieve desegregation.

1986 Congress reauthorizes the Higher Education Act, allocating $100 million for historically black schools.

1989 President George H. W. Bush issues an executive order designed to strengthen the ability of black schools to provide quality educations.

1994 The federal government issues grants to 28 historically black colleges for the purpose of revitalizing their communities.

There are 103 historically black colleges and universities in 20 states and the District of Columbia. The following are listed by state, type, and date of founding.

ALABAMA
Alabama A&M University
(public, four-year, 1875)
Alabama State University
(public, four-year, 1874)
Bishop State Community College
(public, two-year, 1927)
C.A. Fredd State Technical College
(public, two-year, 1965)
Concordia College
(private, two-year, 1961)
J.F. Drake Technical College
(public, two-year, 1961)
Lawson State Community College
(public, two-year, 1965)
Miles College
(private, two-year, 1896)
Oakwood College
(private, two-year, 1896)
Selma University
(private, two-year, 1878)
Stillman College
(private, four-year, 1876)
Talladega College
(private, four-year, 1867)
Trenholm State Technical College
(public, two-year, 1963)
Tuskegee University
(private, four-year, 1881)

ARKANSAS
Arkansas Baptist College
(private, four-year, 1884)
Philander Smith Collge
(private, four-year, 1877)
Shorter College
(private, two-year, 1886)
University of Arkansas
at Pine Bluff
(public, four-year, 1873)

DELAWARE
Delaware State University
(public, four-year, 1891)

DISTRICT OF COLUMBIA
Howard University
(private, four-year, 1867)
University of the District of Columbia
(private, four-year, 1851)

FLORIDA
Bethune-Cookman College
(private, four-year, 1904)
Edward Waters College
(private, four-year, 1866)
Florida A&M University
(public, four-year, 1877)
Florida Memorial College
(private, four-year, 1879)

GEORGIA
Albany State College
(public, four-year, 1903)
Clark Atlanta University
(private, four-year, 1989)
Fort Valley State College
(public, four-year, 1895)
Interdenominational Theological Center
(private, four-year, 1958)
Morehouse College
(private, four-year, 1867)
Morehouse School of Medicine
(private, four-year, 1975)
Morris Brown College
(private, four-year, 1881)
Paine College
(private, four-year, 1890)
Savannah State College
(public, four-year, 1890)
Spelman College
(private, four-year, 1881)

KENTUCKY
Kentucky State University
(public, four-year, 1886)

LOUISIANA
Dillard University
(private, four-year, 1869)
Grambling State University
(public, four-year, 1901)
Southern University A&M College–
Baton Rouge
(public, four-year, 1880)
Southern University at New Orleans
(public, four-year, 1959)
Southern University at Shreveport–
Bossier City
(public, two-year, 1964)
Xavier University of Louisiana
(private, four-year, 1915)

MARYLAND
Bowie State University
(public, four-year, 1865)
Coppin State University
(public, four-year, 1900)
Morgan State University
(public, four-year, 1867)
University of Maryland–
Eastern Shore
(public, four-year, 1886)

MICHIGAN
Lewis College of Business
(private, two-year, 1874)

MISSISSIPPI
Alcorn State University
(public, four-year, 1871)
Coahoma Community College
(public, two-year, 1949)
Hinds Community College
(public, two-year, 1954)
Jackson State University
(public, four-year, 1877)

Mary Holmes College
(private, four-year, 1866)
Tougaloo College
(private, four-year, 1869)

MISSOURI
Harris-Stowe State College
(public, four-year, 1857)
Lincoln University
(public, four-year, 1866)

NORTH CAROLINA
Barber-Scotia College
(private, four-year, 1867)
Bennett College
(private, four-year, 1873)
Elizabeth City State University
(public, four-year, 1891)
Fayetteville State University
(public, four-year, 1877)
Johnson C. Smith University
(private, four-year, 1867)
Livingstone College
(private, four-year, 1879)
North Carolina A&T State University
(public, four-year, 1891)
North Carolina Central University
(public, four-year, 1910)
St. Augustine's College
(private, four-year, 1867)
Shaw University
(private, four-year, 1865)
Winston-Salem State University
(public, four-year, 1862)

OHIO
Central State University
(public, four-year, 1887)
Wilberforce University
(private, four-year, 1856)

OKLAHOMA
Langston University
(public, four-year, 1856)

PENNSYLVANIA

Cheyney University
(public, four-year, 1837)
Lincoln University
(public, four-year, 1854)

SOUTH CAROLINA

Allen University
(private, four-year, 1870)
Benedict College
(private, four-year, 1870)
Claflin College
(private, four-year, 1869)
Clinton Junior College
(private, two-year, 1894)
Denmark Technical College
(public, two-year, 1948)
Morris College
(private, four-year, 1908)
South Carolina State University
(public, four-year, 1896)
Voorhees College
(private, four-year, 1897)

TENNESSEE

Fisk University
(private, four-year, 1867)
Knoxville College
(private, four-year, 1875)
Lane College
(private, four-year, 1882)
LeMoyne-Owen College
(private, four-year, 1862)
Meharry Medical College
(private, four-year, 1876)
Tennessee State University
(public, four-year, 1912)

TEXAS

Huston-Tillotson College
(private, four-year, 1876)
Jarvis Christian College
(private, four-year, 1912)
Paul Quinn College
(private, four-year, 1872)
Prairie View A&M College
(public, four-year, 1876)
Saint Phillip's College
(public, two-year, 1927)
Southwestern Christian College
(private, four-year, 1949)
Texas College
(private, four-year, 1984)
Texas Southern University
(public, four-year, 1947)
Wiley College
(private, four-year, 1873)

VIRGINIA

Hampton University
(private, four-year, 1868)
Norfolk State University
(public, four-year, 1935)
Saint Paul's College
(private, four-year, 1888)
Virginia State University
(public, four-year, 1882)
Virginia Union University
(private, four-year, 1865)

WEST VIRGINIA

Bluefield State College
(public, four-year, 1895)
West Virginia State College
(public, four-year, 1891)

Source: Urban Education, November 2001

Predominately black colleges resemble HBCUs in that they educate large numbers of black students. While HBCUs are federally designated, a predominately black school refers to any institution with 50 percent or greater black enrollment. There are currently 43 predominately black colleges and universities. They are listed below.

ALABAMA

Wallace Community College–
Sparks Campus
(public, two-year, 1927)
John M. Patterson State
Technical College
(public, two-year, 1962)
Reid State Technical College
(public, two-year, 1963)

CALIFORNIA

Charles R. Drew University of
Medicine & Science
(private, four-year, 1966)
Compton Community College
(public, two-year, 1927)
Los Angeles Southwest College
(public, two-year, 1967)
West Los Angeles College
(public, two-year, 1968)

DISTRICT OF COLUMBIA

Southeastern University
(private, four-year, 1879)

GEORGIA

Albany Technical Institute
(public, two-year, 1974)
Atlanta Metropolitan College
(public, two-year, 1974)
Bauder College
(private, two-year, 1964)
Columbus Technical College
(public, two-year, 1961)
DeKalb Technical College
(public, two-year, 1961)

Georgia Military College–
August-Fort Gordon Campus
(public, two-year, 1879)
Georgia Military College–
Fort McPherson Campus
(public, two-year, 1879)
Gupton Jones College of
Funeral Service
(private, two-year, 1920)
Herzing College–Atlanta
(private, four-year, 1949)
Central Georgia Technical College
(public, two-year, 1989)
Savannah Technical College
(public, two-year, 1929)

ILLINOIS

Chicago State University
(public, four-year, 1867)
East St. Louis Community College
(public, two-year, 1969)
East-West University
(private, four-year, 1935)
Kennedy-King College
(public, two-year, 1935)
Malcolm X College
(public, two-year, 1968)
Olive-Harvey College
(public, two-year, 1970)

INDIANA

Martin University
(private, four-year, 1873)

KENTUCKY

Simmons University
(private, four-year, 1873)

MARYLAND
Baltimore City Community College
(public, two-year, 1947)
Prince George's Community College
(public, two-year, 1958)
Sojourner-Douglass College
(private, four-year, 1972)

MASSACHUSETTS
Roxbury Community College
(public, two-year, 1973)

MICHIGAN
Davenport University Dearborn
(private, four-year, 2000)
Davenport University Flint
(private, four-year, 2000)
Wayne County Community College
(public, two-year, 1967)

MISSISSIPPI
East Mississippi Community College
(public, two-year, 1927)
Mississippi Delta Community College
(public, two-year, 1927)
Natchez Junior College
(private, two-year, 1884)

NEW JERSEY
Bloomfield College
(private, four-year, 1868)
Essex County College
(public, two-year, 1966)

NEW YORK
Audrey Cohen College
(private, four-year, 1964)
Fiorello H. LaGuardia
Community College
(public, two-year, 1971)
Helen Fuld College of Nursing
of North General Hospital
(private, two-year, 1945)

Long Island College Hospital
School of Nursing
(private, two-year, 1858)
Medgar Evers College
(public, four-year, 1867)
New York City Technical College
(public, two-year, 1971)
York College
(public, four-year, 1866)

NORTH CAROLINA
Edgecombe Community College
(public, two-year, 1967)
Roanoke-Chowan Community College
(public, two-year, 1967)

OHIO
Cuyahoga Community College
(public, two-year, 1963)

PENNSYLVANIA
Peirce College
(private, four-year, 1865)

SOUTH CAROLINA
Williamsburg Technical College
(public, two-year, 1969)

TENNESSEE
Southwest Tennessee Community College
(public, two-year, 2000)

TEXAS
Bay Ridge Christian College
(private, two-year, 1962)

U.S. VIRGIN ISLANDS
University of the Virgin Islands
(public, four-year, 1962)

VIRGINIA
Virginia University at Lynchburg
(private, four-year, 1888)

Source: Urban Education, November 2001

Barnes, Esmeralda. "Many of America's Tiniest HBCUs Make the Most Colossal Strides in Clearning the Path to College for Underprivileged Youth." *Black Issues in Higher Education*, 27 August 27 1992.

"Booker T. Washington." *World Book.* *http://www2.worldbook.com/features/aajourney/html/bh065.html*

Brown II, M. Christopher, Donahoo, Saran, and Bertrand, Ronyelle, D. "The Black College and the Quest for Educational Opportunity." *Urban Education*, November 2001.

Cheyney University *http://www.cheyney.edu*

Clayborne, Carson, ed. *The Autobiography of Martin Luther King Jr.* New York: Warner Books, 1998.

Clift, Virgil A., Anderson, Archibald W., and Hullfish, H. Gordon (eds.). *Negro Education in America; Its Adequacy, Problems, and Needs.* New York, Harper, 1962.

"College History." Spelman College. *http://www.spelman.edu/registrar/catalog/collegehistory.pdf*

Committee L on the Historically Black Institutions. "The Historically Black Colleges and Universities: A Future in the Balance." *Academe*, January/February 1995.

Douglass, Frederick. *Narrative of the Life of Frederick Douglass, An American Slave.* Berkeley Digital Site. *http://sunsite.berkeley.edu/Literature/Douglass/Autobiography/01.html*

Drewry, Henry N. and Doermann, Humphrey. *Stand and Prosper: Private Black Colleges and Their Students.* Princeton: Princeton University Press, 2001.

DuBois, W.E.B. *The Education of Black People: Ten Critiques.* New York: Monthly Review Press, 2001.

DuBois, W.E.B. "The Freedmen's Bureau." *The Atlantic Monthly*, March 1901.

DuBois, W.E.B. *The Souls of Black Folk.* Grand Rapids, MI: Candace Press, 1996.

Eells, Walter Crosby and Hollis, Ernest V. "Origin and Development of the Public College in the United States." *The Journal of Negro Education*, Summer 1962.

Encyclopedia of Slavery. *http://www.spartacus.schoolnet.co.uk/USAslavery.htm*

Freeman, Kassie and Cohen, Rodney. "Bridging the Gap Between Economic Development and Cultural Empowerment: HBCU's Challenges For the Future." *Urban Education*, November 2001.

Garibaldi, Antoine , ed. *Black Colleges and Universities: Challenges for the Future.* New York: Praeger, 1984.

The Gilder Lehrman Institute of American History. *www.gliah.uh.edu*

Hare, Nathan. "Behind the Black College Revolt." *Ebony.*

Harlan, Louis R. "About Booker T. Washington (1856-1915)." University of North Carolina at Chapel Hill Libraries. *http://docsouth.unc.edu/washington/about.html*

Henderson, Vivian. "The Role of Predominately Negro Institutions." *The Journal of Negro Education.*

Hoffman, Charlene M., Snyder, Thomas D., and Sonnenber, Bill. *Historically Black Colleges and Universities, 1976-1994.* Washington, D.C.: U.S. Dept. of Education, Office of Educational Research and Improvement, 1996.

Holmes, Dwight Oliver Wendell. *The Evolution of the Negro College.* New York, AMS Press, 1970.

Johnson, Charles. *The Negro College Graduate.* New York: Negro Universities Press, 1969.

Kamerstein, Gregory. "Black Colleges: Self-Concept."

Martin, Thad. "Private Black Colleges: Struggle Against the Odds." *Ebony,* October 1983.

McGill, Ralph. "W.E.B. DuBois." *The Atlantic Monthly,* November 1965.

Nelson, William Stuart. "Can Negro Colleges Meet the Challenge of the Modern World?" *Negro Digest,* June 1963.

Phillip, Mary-Christine and Morgan, Joan. "The Morehouse Mystique." *Black Issues in Higher Education,* 16 December 1993.

Ralston, Richard. "The Role of the Black University in the Black Revolution." *The Journal of Black Studies,* March 1973.

Richter, Jay. "The Origin and Development of the Land-Grant College in the United States." *The Journal of Negro Education,* Summer 1962.

"The Richest Black Colleges." *Ebony,* November 1997.

Robinson, Harry G. III and Edwards, Hazel Ruth. *The Long Walk: The Placemaking Legacy of Howard University.* Howard University, 1996.

Roebuck, Julian B. and Murty, Komanduri S., eds. *Historically Black Colleges and Universities: Their Place in American Higher Education.* Westport, Conn.: Praeger, 1993.

Rudwick, Elliott. "Du Bois, W(illiam) E(dward) B(urghardt)."

The Encyclopedia Britannica Guide to Black History. *http://blackhistory.eb.com/micro/179/2.html*

Suggs, Ernie. "A School Without Peer." *The Herald-Sun*, 12 February 1997.

Suggs, Ernie. "An Old-Fashioned Education." *The Herald-Sun*, 11 February, 1997.

Suggs, Ernie. "Getting By On Faith Alone." *The Herald Sun*, 12 February 1997.

Suggs, Ernie. "Invisible Colleges." *The Herald-Sun*, 9 February 1997.

"W.E.B. DuBois: The Man & His Works." University of Pennsylvania. *http://dolphin.upenn.edu/~souls/dubois.htm*

Washington, Booker T. "The Awakening of the Negro." *The Atlantic Monthly*, September 1896.

Washington, Booker T. *Up From Slavery*. Grand Rapids, MI: Candace Press, 1996.

Wenglinsky, Harold. "Historically Black Colleges and Universities: Their Aspirations and Accomplishments." Educational Testing Service, 1999.

Williams, Sharon. "How Did Howard University, One of the Leading Historically Black Colleges and Universities, Develop as an Academic Institution During the Period 1967 Through 1997?" The Association for the Study of Higher Education Conference, 2000.

Wintergreen/Orchard House, Inc. *Historically Black Colleges and Universities*. New York, NY: Macmillan, 1995.

Clift, Virgil A., Anderson, Archibald W., and Hullfish, H. Gordon (eds.). *Negro Education in America; Its Adequacy, Problems, and Needs.* New York, Harper, 1962.

Drewry, Henry N. and Doermann, Humphrey. *Stand and Prosper: Private Black Colleges and Their Students.* Princeton: Princeton University Press, 2001.

DuBois, W.E.B. *The Education of Black People: Ten Critiques.* New York: Monthly Review Press, 2001.

DuBois, W.E.B. *The Souls of Black Folk.* Grand Rapids, MI: Candace Press, 1996.

Garibaldi, Antoine, ed. *Black Colleges and Universities: Challenges for the Future.* New York: Praeger, 1984.

Hoffman, Charlene M., Snyder, Thomas D., and Sonnenber, Bill. *Historically Black Colleges and Universities, 1976-1994.* Washington, D.C.: U.S. Dept. of Education, Office of Educational Research and Improvement, 1996.

Holmes, Dwight Oliver Wendell. *The Evolution of the Negro College.* New York, AMS Press, 1970.

Roebuck, Julian B. and Murty, Komanduri S., eds. *Historically Black Colleges and Universities: Their Place in American Higher Education.* Westport, Conn.: Praeger, 1993.

Willie, Charles V. and Ronald R. Edmonds, eds. *Black Colleges in America: Challenge, Development, Survival.* New York: Teachers College Press, 1978.

Wintergreen/Orchard House, Inc. *Historically Black Colleges and Universities.* New York, NY: Macmillan, 1995.

Washington, Booker T. *Up From Slavery.* Grand Rapids, MI: Candace Press, 1996.

Educational On-Line
http://www.edonline.com/cq/hbcu/

HBCU-Central
http://www.hbcu-central.com/

SmartNet
http://www.smart.net/~pope/hbcu/hbculist.htm

page:
6: © Bettmann/CORBIS
11: Library of Congress, Prints & Photo-
    graphs Diivision, LC-USZ62-59187
15: © Bettmann/CORBIS
16: AP/Wide World Photos
21: Hulton Archive/Getty Images
24: AP/Wide World Photos
28: © CORBIS
31: © CORBIS
34: © Bettmann/CORBIS
39: Library of Congress, Prints & Photo-
    graphs Division, LC-USZ62-64712
42: Hulton Archive/Getty Images
45: © Bettmann/CORBIS
48: Library of Congress, Prints & Photo-
    graphs Division, LC-USZ62-38147

53: Library of Congress, Prints & Photo-
    graphs Division, LC-USZ62-118916
56: © Hulton-Deutsh Collection/
    CORBIS
58: Hulton Archive/Getty Images
63: AP/Wide World Photos
67: AP/Wide World Photos
70: © Bettmann/CORBIS
76: © Bettmann/CORBIS
80: © John Van Hassalt/CORBIS
    SYGMA
84: Hulton Archive/Getty Images
89: © CORBIS
92: © Bettmann/CORBIS
97: AP/Wide World Photos

Cover: © James L. Amos/CORBIS
Frontis: © John Van Hassalt/CORBIS SYGMA

Jennifer Peltak is a 1992 graduate of Temple University in Philadelphia with a degree in journalism. She has been an editor and reporter at newspapers in northern Virginia, and now manages a web site for an educational non-profit organization. She resides in Washington, D.C. This is her second book for Chelsea House.